CLASSROOM TECHNIQUES FOR CREATING CONDITIONS FOR RIGOROUS INSTRUCTION

CLASSROOM TECHNIQUES FOR CREATING CONDITIONS FOR RIGOROUS INSTRUCTION

Jennifer A. Cleary, Terry A. Morgan, Robert J. Marzano

1400 Centrepark Blvd., Ste 1000
West Palm Beach, FL 33401
717.845.6300
email: pub@learningsciences.com
learningsciences.com

Printed in the United States of America
22 21 20 19 18   1 2 3 4 5

FSC
www.fsc.org
MIX
Paper from
responsible sources
FSC® C011935

Library of Congress Control Number: 2017961029

Publisher's Cataloging-in-Publication Data
provided by Five Rainbows Cataloging Services

Names: Cleary, Jennifer, author. | Morgan, Terry, author. | Marzano, Robert J., author.

Title: Classroom techniques for creating conditions for rigorous instruction / Jennifer Cleary, Terry Morgan, [and] Robert J. Marzano.

Description: West Palm Beach, FL : Learning Sciences, 2018. | Series: Essentials for achieving rigor.

Identifiers: LCCN 2017961029 | ISBN 9781943920877 (pbk.) | ISBN 9781943920068 (ebook)

Subjects: LCSH: Teaching Methodology. | Effective teaching. | Education-Standards. | Learning strategies. | BISAC: EDUCATION / Teaching Methods & Materials / General. | EDUCATION / Professional Development. | EDUCATION / Standards.

Classification: LCC LB1025.3 .C54 2017 (print) | LCC LB1025.3 (ebook) | DDC 371.102dc23.

MARZANO CENTER

Essentials for Achieving Rigor SERIES

Other books in the series:

Dedication

To my two greatest influences in life, Mommy and Stu:

Mommy—Thanks for always being there and listening, even when I wasn't hearable. Thank you for teaching me to never quit and, most of all, for being my best friend.

Stu—I know you can see this! Thank you for being my academic role model and for gifting me with the love of learning. "You Should Be Here . . ." —Cole Swindell

—Jennifer Cleary

To my Savior, I am nothing without you. To my wife and kids, you are my heart. To the teachers: You made success possible. I am eternally grateful for your commitment to all kids.

—Terry Morgan

Visit www.learningsciences.com/bookresources
to download reproducibles from this book.

Table of Contents

Acknowledgments

Learning Sciences International would like to thank the following reviewers:

Traci Lowe
Two-time Florida Forensic League Coach of the Year
West Palm Beach, FL

Amber Elder
ELA Coordinator and Putnam City Teacher of the Year
Oklahoma City, OK

About the Authors

ROBERT J. MARZANO, PhD, is a nationally recognized education researcher, speaker, trainer, and author of more than forty books and three hundred articles on topics such as instruction, assessment, writing and implementing standards, cognition, effective leadership, and school intervention. His practical translations of the most current research and theory into classroom strategies are widely practiced internationally by both teachers and administrators.

Dr. Marzano co-developed the Learning Sciences Marzano Center Essentials for Achieving Rigor, a model of instruction that fosters essential teaching skills and strategies to support college and career readiness standards. Dr. Marzano has also partnered with Learning Sciences International (LSI) to offer the Marzano Teacher Evaluation Model, the Marzano School Leadership Evaluation Model, and the Marzano District Leader Evaluation Model.

Dr. Marzano received his doctorate from the University of Washington. Learn more about Dr. Marzano's research, as well as his products and services, at the Learning Sciences Marzano Center, www.MarzanoCenter.com.

JENNIFER A. CLEARY, MEd, earned her bachelor of science in business management from West Chester University of Pennsylvania and completed her education coursework at University of Pennsylvania before moving to Florida to begin her teaching career. After spending several years teaching primary and intermediate students, she earned her master's degree in curriculum and instruction from Concordia University, Portland, Oregon. Ms. Cleary shifted her focus to elementary curriculum and instructional coaching support in the curriculum department at the district level. Her passion for education, curriculum, and student growth led her to LSI, where she currently works in content development and product management. Through this work, Ms. Cleary has had the opportunity to work with educators throughout the country in the pursuit of high-quality rigorous instruction that results in increased student achievement for all.

TERRY A. MORGAN serves as a senior staff developer with LSI, where he has trained in more than twenty-five districts with more than ten thousand teachers from elementary school to the collegiate level. Mr. Morgan's teaching experiences span the K–12 spectrum in the areas of math, science, health, and physical education, and he has served as an instructional specialist in Saint Lucie County, Florida. As an innovative educator and speaker, his work with teachers, schools, and districts has been the foundation and catalyst for growth in both teacher effectiveness and student achievement. Mr. Morgan's new concentration is transforming schools that support economically disadvantaged students.

Introduction

This guide, *Classroom Techniques for Creating Conditions for Rigorous Instruction*, is intended as a resource for improving a specific aspect of instructional practice: creating conditions for learning.

Your motivation to incorporate these strategies into your instructional toolbox may have come from a personal desire to improve your instructional practice through implementation of a research-based set of strategies (such as those found in the Marzano Teacher Evaluation Framework) or a desire to increase the rigor of the instructional strategies you implement in your class so that students meet the expectations of demanding standards such as College and Career Readiness Standards, Next Generation Science Standards, College, Career, and Civic Life (C3) Framework for Social Studies State Standards, or state standards based on or influenced by College and Career Readiness Anchor Standards.

This guide will help teachers of all grade levels and subjects improve their performances of specific instructional strategies designed to create conditions for rigorous instruction, such as establishing rules and procedures, recognizing adherence and lack of adherence to rules and procedures, using engagement strategies when students are not engaged, establishing and maintaining effective relationships, and communicating high expectations for all students. The guide allows you to intentionally plan, implement, monitor, adapt, and reflect on elements of your instructional practice. A person seeking to become an expert displays distinctive behaviors, as explained by Marzano and Toth (2013):

- Breaks down the specific skills required to be an expert

- Focuses on improving those particular critical skill chunks (as opposed to easy tasks) during practice or day-to-day activities

- Receives immediate, specific, and actionable feedback, particularly from a more experienced coach

- Continually practices each critical skill at more challenging levels with the intention of mastering it, giving far less time to skills already mastered

The series of Essentials for Achieving Rigor guides will support each of the above-listed behaviors, with a focus on breaking down the specific skills required to be an expert, and give day-to-day practical suggestions to enhance these skills.

Building on the Marzano Instructional Framework

This series is based on the Marzano Instructional Framework, which is grounded in research and provides educators with the tools they need to connect instructional practice to student achievement. The series uses key terms that are specific to the Marzano model of instruction. Table I.1 provides a glossary of these key terms.

Table I.1: Key Concepts and Terms

Term	Definition
CCSS	Common Core State Standards is the official name of the standards documents developed by the Common Core State Standards Initiative (CCSSI), the goal of which is to prepare America's students for college and career.
CCR	College and Career Readiness Anchor Standards are broad statements that incorporate individual standards for various grade levels and specific content areas.
Desired result	The intended result for the student(s) due to the implementation of a specific strategy.
Monitoring	The act of checking for evidence of the desired result of a specific strategy while the strategy is being implemented.
Instructional strategy	A category of techniques used for classroom instruction that has been proven to have a high probability of enhancing student achievement.
Instructional technique	The method used to teach and deepen understanding of knowledge and skills.
Content	The knowledge and skills necessary for students to demonstrate standards.
Scaffolding	A purposeful progression of support that targets cognitive complexity and student autonomy to reach rigor.
Extending	Activities that move students who have already demonstrated the desired result to a higher level of understanding.

The educational pendulum swings widely from decade to decade. Educators move back and forth between prescriptive checklists and step-by-step lesson plans to approaches that encourage instructional autonomy with minimal regard for the science of teaching and need for accountability. Two practices are often missing in both of these approaches to defining effective instruction: (1) specific statements of desired results, and (2) solid research-based instructional strategies. Launching from the solid instructional foundation of the Marzano Instructional Model, teachers will then be prepared to merge that science with their own unique, yet effective, instructional type, which is the art of teaching.

Classroom Techniques for Creating Conditions for Rigorous Instruction will help you grow into an innovative and highly skilled teacher who is able to implement, scaffold, and extend instruction to meet a range of student needs.

Essentials for Achieving Rigor

This series of guides details essential classroom strategies to support the complex shifts in teaching that are necessary for an environment where academic rigor is a requirement for all students. The instructional strategies presented in this series are essential to effectively teach the CCR, the Next Generation Science Standards, or standards designated by your school district or state. They require a deeper understanding, more effective use of strategies, and greater frequency of implementation for your students to demonstrate the knowledge and skill required by rigorous standards. This series includes instructional techniques appropriate for all grade levels and content areas. The examples contained within are grade-level specific and should serve as models and launching points for application in your own classroom.

Your skillful implementation of these strategies is essential to your students' mastery of the CCR or other rigorous standards, no matter the grade level or subject matter you are teaching. Instructional strategies such as those found within this series of books help exemplify the cognitive complexity needed to meet rigorous standards. Taken as a package, these strategies may at first glance seem quite daunting. That is why this series focuses on just one strategy—or in this case, one concept—in each guide.

Chapter 1

CONDITIONS FOR RIGOROUS INSTRUCTION

Rigorous instruction and learning do not just happen by accident or by coincidence. In order for rigorous instruction to consistently occur in your classroom, you must pay close attention to the learning environment. In fact, one could argue that before planning to instruct any content at all, it is imperative to plan for the conditions within the learning environment. Without the appropriate conditions in place, consistent levels of rigorous instruction, learning, and performance are unachievable.

As teachers, you are continuously building relationships with (and between) your students, whether you are conscious of it or not. Your teaching methods, routines, engagement strategies, and expectations speak to your students all of the time. The focus for this guide is planning for and creating an environment that is optimal for rigorous instruction, learning, and ultimately, student success.

When creating conditions for learning, it is important to pay close attention to the needs of your students. English language learners (ELLs), students who receive special education, and students who lack support for school all come with their own unique sets of needs. Supporting these individual needs starts with the learning environment.

Often these needs are the direct result of societal issues such as poverty, which is a growing issue in the United States. Students living in poverty are likely to lack resources, including financial, emotional, mental, spiritual, and physical resources. They may also lack support systems, relationships, role models, and knowledge of hidden rules. Lacking these resources may directly affect academic achievement (Rowan et al., 2004). It is critical to ensure that societal issues do not determine the achievement of students. According to Shields (1991), there are three key factors that affect student learning: the school environment, the home or community environment, and the policies of the district or state. Although external conditions play a significant role in students' lives outside of school, we can control the conditions created within the school environment and ultimately harness them to influence learning. Good conditions have a positive impact on the student's brain, achievement, and development.

By establishing effective conditions for learning, teachers possess the ability to overcome student impediments to learning despite their root causes. Kati Haycock of the Education Trust puts it this way: The research indicates that students who have strong teachers over multiple years in a row will eventually excel regardless of their backgrounds. Students who receive instruction from just two weak teachers in a row will continue to struggle (Peske & Haycock, 2006). Positive experiences with strong teachers can break the cycle of adverse experiences associated with any and all high-risk root causes. The conditions established for learning inside the classroom can provide students with experiences that are not had elsewhere and create the environment for students to experience emotional, social, and academic success (Jensen, 2009).

Not only does creating conditions for the learning environment allow us to impact students with various needs, but it also allows us to push all of our students to rigor. Rigor is achieved by increasing cognitive complexity and student autonomy of essential knowledge and skills. Rigor cannot be achieved without both cognitive complexity and student autonomy (figure 1.1).

Creating conditions for learning in the classroom and ensuring that the conditions are functioning at a quality level afford the teacher greater ability to increase the cognitive complexity of instruction and learning. Because these conditions are in place, strategies are easily accessed and applied to enhance the classroom learning environment.

Besides impacting cognitive complexity, establishing conditions for learning also provides the necessary structure to ensure autonomy for all students. The learning environment must be facilitated in such a way that every student is pushed to achieve rigorous standards. In many schools, the achievement gap is most pronounced in thinking at higher levels of Marzano's Taxonomy, including deriving meaning from text, drawing inferences, and understanding rate and measurement in mathematics (Noguera, 2012). When student

Figure 1.1: Rigor in a standards-based classroom must contain high levels of both cognitive complexity and student autonomy. The dot marks the sweet spot where rigor lives.

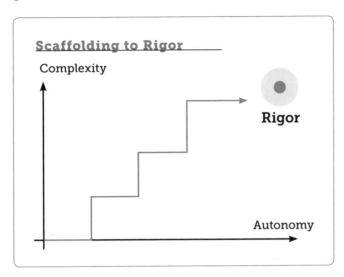

autonomy is lagging, it can often be traced back to the conditions of the learning environment. For rigor to be achieved, student autonomy and cognitive complexity must be attainable for all students. The research-based conditions discussed in this guide serve to do just that.

Effective Implementation of Establishing Conditions for Rigorous Instruction

As discussed in the previous section, the need for establishing conditions for rigorous instruction is twofold. When effective conditions have not been established, student behaviors can be misclassified as emotional or learning disabilities. Effective conditions also provide the environment for achieving rigor in the classroom. These conditions provide the environment for cognitive complexity, as well as enhance instruction, when they are in place. As teachers push to foster student autonomy, conditions must be in place to ensure that all students are advancing. As you move through this guide, you will focus on five strategies. Within each strategy, you will discover multiple techniques for implementation.

The intention of rigorous instruction is to prepare students to be productive members of an ever-changing society. The skills necessary for participation in the twenty-first-century classroom are vastly different from those in the past. College and Career Readiness Standards require that specific mental skills and processes are directly taught to students and fostered in the context of regular classroom instruction. They are categorized into two broad categories: cognitive skills and conative skills. Cognitive skills are those we are most familiar with in education. They are the ability to think about new information, process it, speak about it, and apply it to other, previously acquired information. Conative skills refer to the ability to examine knowledge and emotions in order to choose an appropriate course of action. These are personality skills involving temperament and emotion. Conative skills are critical for an individual to successfully engage in self-direction and self-regulation. Embedded in the strategies are conative skills, which are necessary for achieving autonomy and ultimately rigor. As you consider how to effectively implement establishing conditions for rigorous instruction, note the following strategies:

- Establishing rules and procedures

- Recognizing adherence and lack of adherence to rules and procedures

- Using engagement strategies when students are not engaged

- Establishing and maintaining effective relationships

- Communicating high expectations for all students

Common Mistakes to Avoid When Establishing Conditions for Rigorous Instruction

As you begin to implement the strategies and techniques involved in creating conditions for learning, consider how to avoid common mistakes. A minor mistake can derail your efforts. The mistakes common to creating conditions for rigor include the following.

Creating an Environment Where Rules Are Used as Punishment

Rules and procedures are a classroom nonnegotiable; they provide structure for the learning environment to increase the probability of achievement. When rules and procedures are used inappropriately, they rob students of the ability to self-regulate. When rules and procedures are provided to students, and students use them to self-regulate, students take ownership of the environment as well. The classroom belongs to the students as much as to the teacher.

Failing to Be Consistent

Remaining consistent is imperative when supporting students, whether the teacher is providing support through instruction or acknowledging adherence and/or lack of adherence to rules and procedures. Consistency in the volume, depth, and type of interaction goes a long way in establishing a learning environment where all students feel their needs are being met.

Failing to Remain Emotionally Objective

There are undoubtedly moments in the classroom that can cause emotional triggers. Teachers must remain emotionally objective in order to create the type of learning environment that supports all students. Remaining objective and keeping emotions in check can go a long way in establishing positive relationships with students.

Failing to Engage Students

In order for any meaningful learning to take place, students must be cognitively engaged. Cognitive engagement requires that students are attending to the instruction. Teachers must realize that it is virtually impossible to have 100 percent cognitive engagement from 100 percent of the students 100 percent of the time. With this being said, an effective teacher continuously monitors the level of engagement and takes action when students are not engaged.

Failing to Establish Positive Relationships

Positive relationships go a long way in the classroom. If the teacher-student relationships are good, there is a decrease in overall disruptions. In fact, it can be said that a good relationship between teacher and students has the power to enhance everything else in the classroom. Conversely, a lot of behavior issues that occur can be directly linked to a poor student-teacher relationship (Marzano, 2007). Therefore, failing to establish positive relationships has the power to negatively impact the level of rigor achieved in the classroom.

Failing to Have High Expectations for All Students

An often unspoken dynamic of classrooms everywhere is the level of expectations a teacher has for each student. Teachers' expectations for their students can dictate the frequency and depth of interactions they have with students. Often an unconscious dynamic, failing to communicate high expectations for all students limits a student's ability to achieve autonomy with rigorous standards.

Opportunities to Teach and Reinforce Conative Skills

As noted previously, conative skills refer to the ability to examine knowledge and emotions in order to choose an appropriate course of action. Conative skills help prepare students to interact with peers and are critical for students to successfully engage in self-direction and self-regulation, which prepare them for college and career. As you examine each strategy for conditions for learning, you will also discover which conative skills can be successfully supported through the use of that specific strategy.

- **Becoming aware of the power of interpretation:** Students become aware that how they interpret a situation influences how they think, feel, and act.

- **Cultivating a growth mindset:** Students come to believe that they are capable of increasing their intelligence or improving their ability.

- **Cultivating resiliency:** Students are able to overcome failure. They face challenges and adversity but continue to persevere.

- **Avoiding negative thinking:** Although emotions are inevitable, students become able to prevent emotions from dictating their thoughts and actions.

- **Taking various perspectives:** Students develop the ability to think beyond their own reasoning while examining multiple or conflicting perspectives on a given topic.

- **Interacting responsibly:** Students become able to interact with peers and become accountable for the outcomes of these interactions.

- **Handling controversy and conflict resolution:** Students become able to react appropriately or positively in a situation where there is conflict or controversy.

Instructional Strategies and Techniques to Help Establish Conditions for Learning

There are many ways to establish conditions for learning. Your ultimate goal is to create a classroom climate in which rigorous instruction and learning are possible. When properly cultivated, these conditions also support students with varying needs. Within each strategy used to establish conditions for learning, there are various methods. These methods are called *techniques*. For each of the strategies discussed in this guide, several techniques are offered for implementation. As we noted earlier, the five strategies for creating conditions for rigorous instruction are:

1. Establishing rules and procedures

2. Recognizing adherence and lack of adherence to rules and procedures

3. Using engagement strategies when students are not engaged

4. Establishing and maintaining effective relationships

5. Communicating high expectations for all students

All of the strategies are similarly organized and include the following components:

- An introduction to the strategy and each technique within

- Ways to effectively implement the strategy and each technique within

- Common mistakes to avoid when implementing the strategy

- Opportunities to teach and reinforce conative skills

- Examples and nonexamples of the strategy in action

- Monitoring for the desired result of each strategy

- Scaffolding and extending instruction to meet students' needs

- Additional resources

Chapter 2

ESTABLISHING RULES AND PROCEDURES

A study conducted by Jacob Kounin showed that effective teachers handled discipline problems no differently than ineffective teachers. What made teachers effective was how they managed their classrooms *before* the misbehavior occurred (Kounin, 1970). In other words, one of the most important steps teachers can take is to establish clear rules and procedures early on. In *The First Days of School*, Wong and Wong (2001) stress the importance of establishing procedures at the beginning of the year and communicating those expectations to students. Managing the classroom before misbehavior occurs has the potential to set the tone of the classroom for the entire year.

The ability of teachers to systematically and clearly establish rules and procedures is critical to the success of establishing effective classroom conditions. According to Marzano (2007), it is impossible for students to be productive without guidelines. Rules and procedures need to be clearly articulated to avoid misinterpretation. Jenson (2009) also stresses the need for teachers to provide structure for students within the school setting. Students may not know the appropriate way to perform or behave in certain school settings due to varied background experiences, which impact the way they see the world. But when teachers establish rules and procedures from the very start, it provides students with identical experiences, thus leveling the playing field for all.

Ways to Effectively Implement Establishing Rules and Procedures

Rules identify general expectations regarding student behavior. *Procedures* communicate expectations for specific behavior, a method or process for accomplishing activities in the classroom. The best time to establish rules and procedures is the beginning of the year. Effective teachers spend a lot of time making sure students fully understand and accept all the behavioral expectations set forth in the rules and procedures. They also take time to explain the rationale behind the rules and procedures, and students practice procedures often enough to execute them in a routine way. Research shows an enhanced effect when teachers ask students for input into the classroom rules and procedures (Marzano, 2007).

There are two techniques for establishing rules and procedures that we will look at in some detail: (1) developing and teaching classroom rules and procedures, and (2) organizing physical space. Classroom rules and procedures provide structure that enhances student learning. Procedures, routines, and the physical layout of the classroom support efficient and effective learning. A classroom may become chaotic due to lack of management—and chaos does not support or enhance learning! When rules and procedures are missing or ineffective, class time may be wasted, student attention will wander, and learning will be inhibited (Marzano, 2007).

Teachers can also model and demonstrate appropriate behavior to reinforce positive behavior outcomes, rather than simply telling students what to do. Following are suggestions to increase the effectiveness of your implementation.

Teaching the Rules and Procedures

Classroom rules and procedures are necessary throughout the course of the day and especially during times that may not seem extremely significant. Some of these moments are:

- Normal classroom time

- Beginning and ending of the day or period

- Transitions (carpet to desks, between classes, going to lunch or special area, etc.)

- Class interruptions

- Acquisition of materials and equipment

- Group work

- Independent seatwork

- Management of student absences

- Reengagement following disruption (bringing back the focus of attention)

- Peer tutoring

- Movement around the room

- Student entry and dismissal

The following techniques create a level playing field during the first days of school. The steps provide students with identical experiences to help them develop a shared understanding and knowledge of rules and procedures, which can help prevent disruptions.

Your rules and procedures may need to be adjusted throughout the year as situations arise. When a rule or procedure fails to produce the desired result, first determine whether the rule or procedure is either (1) not effective or (2) unnecessary. If unnecessary, discard the rule or procedure. If the rule or procedure is not yielding the desired result, carry out the following process.

Explain Rules and Procedures

State each rule or procedure *and* explain the rationale for each.

"One of our 'Very Important Rules' is to always walk in the classroom. The reason this rule is important is because we have a lot of students, furniture, and other items in the classroom. If everyone follows the walking-only rule, it is a lot less likely that someone will get hurt. When we run, we have a smaller chance of seeing furniture that may be out of place or other students moving in front of us. Accidents happen, but if we are all walking, they are less likely. So, this rule is important because it keeps us all safe."

> "One important classroom rule that I will emphatically support this year is that everyone must walk at all times. Take a look around this lab. There are Bunsen burners, sharp objects, and other potential hazards. Along with only using these tools as they are intended, always walking in this classroom will help keep us all safe."

Rehearse

Have students practice the rules and procedures under supervision.

> "Now that I have introduced the new rule, let's practice. Since we are all on the carpet, when I say go, I would like for each of you to return to your seat in a safe manner. That means that you will walk back to your seats. Ready? Now, return to your seats."

> "Keeping in mind the rules we just discussed, I'd like you to each retrieve your lab notebook and return to your seat with your partner. I'll be watching to make sure that everyone is following the rules. If there are no questions, please go get your notebooks."

Reinforce

Reteach the rules and procedures, rehearse them, and practice them until they become habits or routines.

"OK, boys and girls. Before we line up, I want to remind you of our 'Very Important Rule' of walking in class. I wanted to bring it to your attention today because I noticed that some of us have been forgetful lately, especially when lining up. So, I stopped a little early today so we could practice. Remember, walking is very important to keep us safe. When I ask you to line up, please do so. And remember to walk. OK, everyone, line up please."

"Today we begin our second lab that requires us to have lots of materials out. Some of the items are sharp, and we will also have chemicals at our tables. It is really important to remember and follow our safety rules. I would hate to see someone get hurt when it could have been avoided. Please use caution and always walk inside the classroom. I've already placed your materials on the windowsill, so when I call your group, please walk to the window, select your materials, and walk back to the table."

Your rules and procedures may differ depending on the instructional strategy you are using during a teaching session. But in any case, these rules need to be clearly articulated, practiced, and reinforced. For example:

- **No conversation versus group conversation.** Does the instructional strategy you are using require students to work in groups? Or are students working independently to produce individual products? Your rules and procedures will vary. For example, when students are working in groups, each member may have a job that ensures each student participates in the learning. These roles will likely require conversation. In contrast, if the intention is for students to work independently, a likely rule will be to keep one's eyes on one's own paper or to refrain from conversations.

- **Sitting at independent desks versus sitting with a group.** Student interactions should look and sound different in each of these settings. For example, the procedure for how completed work is collected for group work versus individual assignments would vary. Perhaps individual work is passed down the line to the left until it reaches the end of the row. In a group, one member may be designated to collect the work of the group and place it in a "finished work" folder near the teacher's desk.

- **Establishing discussion procedures.** Students should understand when it is acceptable to call out an answer or wait their turn to respond. At times during the instructional day, each procedure is appropriate and necessary. The important point here is that both the students and the teacher know when each action is appropriate.

- **No product versus product from group discussion.** This example may seem more obvious than others, but there should be one set of rules and procedures for the production and presentation of written work and another set for the product of a group discussion. If there is a product, the rule may state that each student identify his or her contribution by placing initials next to the section or use software that tracks each member's contribution. For group discussions, each member might be required to participate a specific number of times during the discussion. The group may track this interaction by placing tokens in the middle of the table upon sharing or by assigning a group recorder.

- **Teacher-directed versus student-directed instruction.** Often, teachers will have different sets of rules and procedures for when they are instructing versus when students are working either independently or in groups. Procedures for visiting the restroom, sharpening a pencil, conferring with peers, and asking for help will vary greatly depending on the instructional setting. The teacher below, for example, is explaining procedures for using the restroom or getting a drink of water, depending on the instructional setting.

"I know that we will all have to use the restroom or get a drink at different times during the day. And I know that I don't like to be told when I can do so. When visiting the restroom or water fountain, I'd like you to consider what is taking place in the classroom. There are many times throughout the day when you will be working independently. That may be during reading or math centers or once I have explained a task and released you to work either independently or in groups. These would be the best times for you to step away. If it is an emergency, and you need to use the restroom while I'm speaking to the whole class, you will need to ask permission by raising your pinky in the air. When I nod at you, you may get up and go. During the times when I am not speaking to the class and you are doing your work, there is no need to ask permission. Simply look to see that no one else is waiting, and you may go. If someone is already at the door, please wait until there is no one waiting."

Additionally, creating acronyms for the important concepts of the rules and procedures might be helpful, such as P-A-C-T-S. At the beginning of the year the teacher tells students that they will have P-A-C-T-S throughout the year for behavior during their lessons. P-A-C-T-S is an agreement, covenant, or compact. You may continue to teach and reinforce the meaning of each letter (Sprick & Baldwin, 2009):

P = Product. What is the goal or product of the activity?

A = Action. What are the rules about movement during this activity?

C = Collaboration. What are the rules about participation during this activity?

T = Talk. What are the rules about talking during this activity?

S = Support. How do I get support or help if I need it?

Organizing Physical Space

A good classroom seating assignment is the cheapest form of classroom management.

—Fred Jensen

When you're planning the organization of your classroom space, the best principle is to *create physical conditions that facilitate and support teaching and learning.* The physical conditions should provide for flexibility in organizing students. We often overlook ways to organize physical space, but it's an important component of designing effective rules and procedures (Marzano, 2007).

Following are some questions to ask yourself when planning to organize physical space:

- **How many students will be in the class?** Managing a large group of students will require a different organizational setup than a smaller group. It's not uncommon to face some limitations in space and furniture, so understanding your resources and being deliberate in the placement is key in successfully organizing the classroom for the number of your students.

- **Will all students be able to easily see the teacher?** The organization of the classroom should take instruction into account. When organizing your classroom, consider the primary location of direct instruction. Does the angle of desks cause some students to strain? Are any students turned away from this primary location? Are any structures blocking the view of the primary location?

- **What are the primary patterns of movement in and around the class?** When organizing your classroom, plan for transitions throughout the day. When will students be required to move around the room? What movement patterns will they follow? Examples of movement around the room could include lining up, using the restroom, switching stations, changing class periods, moving to collaborative groups, etc.

- **What arrangement is best for students to focus on learning during each segment of the lesson?** If the organization of the classroom must change to support particular segments of the lesson, it helps if the initial organization provides a means for simple movement or transition. Minor rearrangement of furniture may be necessary, but if the rearrangement causes disruption, you may want to reconsider the initial organization. For example, in a primary classroom, it may be beneficial to instruct the whole group with students all sitting in one place, such as the carpet, and then send them back to their desks for independent or group work. As long as the routine is taught, this is a simple transition requiring minimal time and disruption. Students simply walk from one area to another. For this to be an orderly transition, the room must be arranged so that traffic patterns are easily established and maneuverable.

With older students, you will still need to have the full attention of the group at times, while other times require independent or group work. During direct instruction, students usually face the instructor or one common point of focus to facilitate student learning. However, when students are asked to transition to independent or group work, their points of focus will change, thus calling for a different classroom arrangement. Organize your classroom so that it is simple to shift furniture with little disruption. Students can learn quickly to shift desks two feet to the right or left or to turn desks to make a group. Regardless of whether they are engaged in grouped, paired, or independent work, you want to ensure that students have easy access to necessary materials and visual cues. Please see the example in figure 2.1.

Figure 2.1: An example of organizing physical space.

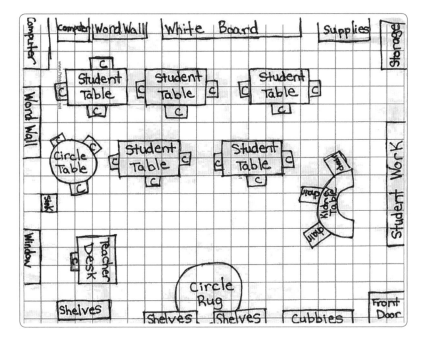

Common Mistakes to Avoid When Establishing Rules and Procedures

Not Planning for Establishing Rules and Procedures

A very common mistake is failing to plan necessary rules and procedures for major as well as seemingly insignificant activities. You may have a plan for students walking in the hallway or using indoor speaking voices, but failing to plan for smaller details such as roles for group work could make or break an activity. How will students access a new pencil when the one they are using breaks? When the teacher says, "Turn in your assignment," what exactly does that mean?

Using Rules and Procedures for Punishment Instead of Structure for Learning

Although it is suggested that consequences occur when one has not complied with a specific rule or procedure, keep in mind that they are not the sole purpose of rules and procedures. The purpose of rules and procedures is to create a structure for learning. The desired result is that students understand classroom rules and procedures, that they can move easily about the classroom, and that they have easy access to materials. If taught, implemented, and practiced effectively, there should be little need for consequences.

Organizing the Room in a Manner That Is Not Conducive to Movement

Even if all other rules and procedures are in place, poor arrangement of physical space could negate their positive effect. If the procedure for turning in assignments includes multiple students walking to the same location at the same time, but the room is not arranged to provide the space for multiple students in that location, trouble could arise. It is important to think about the traffic patterns, student grouping, and visibility when organizing physical space.

It is important not only for students to move about the classroom but also the teacher. All students should be accessible within just a few steps. If you find it necessary to step over or squeeze past students, furniture, or materials, consider rearranging the learning space.

Opportunities to Teach and Reinforce Conative Skills

Remember, conative skills enable students to make proper real-world decisions, combining emotion and intelligence in order to come to a conclusion. Conative and cognitive skills work together in a rigorous classroom.

Interacting Responsibly

Responsible interactions between students are conative skills that support classroom rules and procedures. Students should be proactive and know that their words and actions have power to positively impact student conversations. Ultimately, productive communication enhances learning. Responsible interaction is determined differently in different settings. Because of this, be sure to share your expectations for interactions with all your students, regardless of their ages. High schoolers may just need verbal reminders to reinforce responsible interaction. In younger grades, students may need to be directly taught and provided with tangible reminders, prompts, or props in order to have continuous reinforcement.

For example, we observed the following instruction in a fourth-grade classroom.

"Your teams are going to participate in a conversation about the text. The prompts have been provided to you. Please remember that it is very important that each member of the team participates in a meaningful way. I have placed your conversation gems at each group of desks, so that when you have a gem to contribute—something meaningful to add to the conversation—you place one of your gems in the discussion jar. Fellow teammates, you are responsible for determining if the contribution truly is a gem or if your teammate needs to elaborate."

As the conversations took place, students could be heard stating, "I have a gem to add to the conversation." Their teammates could also be heard reminding them to add to the conversation or prompting them with statements such as, "Amy, you haven't put a gem in the bucket in a while. Do you have something to add?"

Handling Controversy and Conflict Resolution

Controversy arises when people disagree about foundational beliefs. When students from varying backgrounds and socioeconomic statuses come to school, they likely arrive with different viewpoints. This in and of itself is not negative. The perceived controversy becomes a potential problem when it creates conflict. Conflict is created when the beliefs of one become an obstacle to another's goal. Rules and procedures create structures and guidelines to allow room for controversy and either eliminate conflict or support its resolution. Controversy and conflict are inevitable. Our preparation for reacting to and resolving them dictates the impact they have on learning. Figure 2.2 offers some examples of rules and procedures for peer interactions and conflict resolution.

Figure 2.2: Discussion template for handling controversy.

In this example, an elementary class is provided with a tangible reminder of responsible interaction. It suggests three ways to respond to other students while offering sentence starters to further elaborate. This discussion template can be applied to handling controversy and conflict resolution as well as interacting responsibly.

Agree	More to Add	Disagree
I agree with _____. I understood that _____ said _____, and I agree. _____ said _____, and there is nothing more to add.	I agree with what _____ is saying, but I would like to add _____. I think that part of the answer is correct, but I would like to add _____. In addition to the points that have been made, _____.	I see your point; however, _____. Since I've listened to your point of view, can I tell you more about mine? I disagree but would like to understand why you say that.

Examples and Nonexamples of Establishing Rules and Procedures

Each of the following examples, one elementary and one secondary, has a corresponding nonexample. Although these examples may come from a grade level or subject area different from the one you teach, consider them, as well as the examples in following chapters, as transferrable and applicable to any grade level.

Elementary Example

The teacher below has planned for every transition for her day. Before school begins, the first-grade teacher identifies all the points in the day that might require rules and procedures to be put in place. She examines transitions, types of interactions her students may have, bathroom policies for different times of day, and many other situations that might require unique sets of rules and procedures. For each of these times, and for each of these rules and procedures, she has planned how she will explain them to students, how students will practice, and how she will reinforce as necessary. Figure 2.3 (page 26) is the planning tool she has created to plan for transitions between centers. See how she begins to teach this procedure, even on the first day of school.

On the first day of school, the teacher is aware that much of her time will be spent explaining and practicing the rules and procedures, and she has done this throughout the day. At this point in the day, her students are working in small groups in designated areas of the room, which will be literacy workstations as time goes on. The volume in the room is just above a whisper, as students have been practicing the appropriate voice level to use during this time. As the voice level increased, the teacher stopped to remind students of the appropriate level and reinforce the rule. Ten minutes before time to clean up and transition to the next subject, she stops and gets the students' attention by raising her hand and waiting for each student to stop work and raise his or her hand as well, signaling that the class is ready to listen for directions. This procedure has been explained and practiced throughout the day. When she has the attention of all of the first graders, she begins to explain the next procedure to her students.

"When it is time for us to clean up, I will ring this bell. All of your stations have materials, and they should be packed up exactly as you found them. This makes it easier to keep track of the materials, and it also helps the next visitors to the station by making it ready for them. Please practice putting your items away now. When you are finished, put your hand back in the air. That will tell me you are ready for the next direction."

Figure 2.3: Planning steps to teach rules and procedures.

Planning the Steps to Teach Rules and Procedures

List the rule or procedure for which you are planning: Procedure for transitioning between Literacy Block and Math.

Record your plans for using the steps of teaching rules and procedures in the space provided below.

Explain the rule or procedure: How will you define and describe the rule/procedure? What rationale will you share with students?

Define / Describe

Rationale:
① Center is ready for the next person.
② Keep track of materials

① Bell ring means clean up.
② Materials packed as you found them.
③ Raise hands when ready for next direction.

Rehearse the rule or procedure: In what activity will your students participate in order to practice the rule or procedure?

End centers early to practice the routine.
Step-by-Step
① Ring bell and wait for attention
② Students clean up materials under super vision / correction
③ Students raise hands to show completion

Continue to practice & monitor: "on-the-job training"

Reinforce the rule or procedure: What specific activities will students use to turn new rules and procedures into habits?

Students will practice the procedure in real-time. The length of time provided at the end of each rotation will diminish over time.

As students practice cleaning up their workstations, the teacher walks around the room and monitors them. As she sees students struggling to follow directions, she quietly reminds them of what they have been asked to do. For the first several weeks of school, she continues to explain, rehearse, and reinforce the rules and procedures throughout the days.

Elementary Nonexample

The nonexample teacher is using the same activity, but he does not follow the three-step process of explaining, practicing, and reinforcing the rules and procedures. It was clear that the previous teacher used this approach with each rule and procedure that led up to the one in the example, and it should become clear that this teacher does not. On the first day of school, he has his first-grade students working in small groups. The noise level is very loud, and it is time to clean up and transition to the next part of the day. In a loud voice, the teacher says, "OK, everyone! It is time to clean up!" Many of the students continue with their conversations, not acknowledging the teacher at all. He has failed to explain or rehearse an attention signal, so students do not know when to stop.

When he has their attention, he simply asks them to clean up and go back to their seats. Some students begin putting items away, others continue their conversations, and others keep working. Some students return to their seats, and some simply wander the classroom. The students are unable to follow the directions because the directions have not been explained to them, nor have they had the opportunity to practice. This causes chaos and lost instructional time.

Secondary Example

On the first day of school, the tenth-grade science teacher has given her first assignment. Students are filling out a questionnaire that will help her to know what students have learned in previous classes. Although the questionnaires will be insightful, she has further plans. When it is time to turn in the assignment, she asks students to put their pencils down and listen as she explains the procedure.

"When I ask you to turn in an assignment, please pass it to your left. If you are the person at the end of the row, raise your hand." She waits to see that all "collectors" know their role. She then continues.

"You are responsible for bringing the assignments in your row to the bin at the front of the room. Please be sure that they are stacked neatly before bringing them up. Walk straight up the aisle to my desk, but then walk back around the room to complete a circle on your way to your seat. The purpose of this is so everyone is not out of their seats at the same time, and if you follow the traffic pattern, there will be no accidents. Most important, you will know that your paper has been received by me, and I will know that everyone has had the opportunity to turn it in."

This teacher uses a humorous traffic metaphor to explain the rationale for her procedure. Once she has reviewed the procedure, she asks the class to practice step-by-step, first passing their questionnaires to the left. The teacher asks the collectors to wait until she gives the next direction. She then directs them to stand and turn the questionnaires in, following the traffic pattern described. As they do this, she watches and makes any necessary corrections to the procedure as needed. The result is an orderly process for turning in assignments, which will last throughout the year.

Secondary Nonexample

In the same classroom as the secondary example above, students are completing a similar questionnaire. They work on this until the bell rings. As students begin to scatter and talk, the teacher calls over them, "Please don't forget to turn in your assignment." Some students bring their papers to the front of the room, leaving them on the teacher's desk, while others run to her, cramming their papers into her hands as they exit. When the room is empty, she is left holding some papers, finding some on her desk, and even finding some on student desks and on the floor.

The students have not been given a procedure to follow, nor have they been told why it might be important to follow one. If this is not rectified, papers and precious instructional time will be lost.

Monitoring for the Desired Result of Establishing Rules and Procedures

Once rules and procedures have been established, determine if your students know and understand them. Consider, as well, if the rules and procedures put in place provide the means for students to move about the classroom and access materials easily. The following suggestions may help:

- Provide classroom scenarios, and ask students to write which rule or procedure the scenario applies to on their whiteboards. Scan whiteboard responses.

> "I've asked the class to pack up their folders and prepare to go home. We know that the bell is going to ring, and everyone is excited for the weekend. Which rule must we all keep in mind? Write or draw the rule on your whiteboard, and be prepared to explain."

- Have students make posters or graphics depicting rules and procedures. Circulate to review student work.

> "I have each rule on a piece of paper in this hat. I will pass the hat, and I would like Person 1 from each group to select a rule. As a team, create a poster or other representation of the rule. I'll walk around, and I should be able to guess the rule you selected. Once I have evidence that you understand the rules, we can hang these in the classroom as reminders."

- Review rules and procedures, and listen as students restate or discuss.

> "I've provided each set of partners with one rule. I am going to walk around and listen as you discuss the rule. I'm listening to hear that you understand the rule, can give an example of when it is necessary, and can explain the purpose of the rule."

Please see the proficiency scale in figure 2.4 to determine your level of proficiency within this strategy.

Figure 2.4: Student proficiency scale for establishing rules and procedures. The proficiency scale identifies phases of implementation regarding the strategy. The "Desired Result" articulates the desired outcome of using the strategy, while "Emerging" and "Fundamental" represent a developmental progression in its use.

Condition	Emerging	Fundamental	Desired Result
Establishing rules and procedures	Identify the purpose for the rules and procedures, including the physical layout of the classroom.	Establish rules and procedures that facilitate students working individually, in groups, and as a whole class, including organizing the physical layout of the classroom.	The desired result of establishing rules and procedures is that all students know classroom rules and procedures, can move easily about the classroom, and have easy access to materials.

Scaffold and Extend to Meet Student Needs

Adjustments in instruction may be required to reach the desired result with students. These adaptations are dependent on the technique being implemented and should provide the extra support, scaffolding, or extensions students may need to reach the desired result.

Scaffolding

- Create a picture for each rule or procedure.

- Tell personal stories.

- Create posters.

- Role-play (teacher participation).

Extending

- Ask students to classify rules and procedures and explain grouping.

- Ask students to role-play.

- Create a class poster summarizing rules and procedures.

- Students use problem-solving skills to resolve a classroom situation.

Remember that your goal in establishing, practicing, and reinforcing rules and procedures is to provide structure that enhances student learning. Your attention to this strategy will help create the conditions to support all students to achieve their best.

Chapter 3

RECOGNIZING ADHERENCE AND LACK OF ADHERENCE TO RULES AND PROCEDURES

As discussed in chapter 2, students may struggle academically due to a lack of awareness of positive behavior that supports learning. In turn, this lack of awareness often leads to consequences such as behavior referrals, removals from class, and suspensions. A study in Texas, "Breaking Schools' Rules" (Fabelo et al., 2012), used information gathered by following incoming seventh graders through three years of school. Over that three-year period, almost 60 percent of the students in the study were suspended at least once, and 31 percent were suspended at least four times. One in seven students in the study was suspended at least eleven times.

The study also found that African American students and students with educational disabilities were much more likely to be removed from classrooms for disciplinary reasons. Pedro Noguera (2012) discusses a similar finding in "The Achievement Gap and the Schools We Need: Creating the Conditions Where Race and Class No Longer Predict Student Achievement," concluding that minority students who come from financially disadvantaged families typically receive a majority of the punishment in school. The correlation may be made that financially disadvantaged students are a statistically overrepresented population being subjected to the harshest forms of discipline. It should be noted, however, that in the case of all students, regardless of background, teachers may take actions to avoid the types of punishments described above.

Of course, teachers do need to apply consequences when students fail to adhere to rules and procedures. Research shows that an effective learning environment requires a balanced approach, one that acknowledges both positive and negative behaviors. In *The Art and Science of Teaching*, Marzano (2007) notes that "rules and procedures for which there are no consequences—positive and negative—do little to enhance learning."

Certainly, students whose behavioral consequences result in exclusion from class do not perform as well as their counterparts. This disparity, in light of the new rigorous standards, sheds light on the unmistakable connection between the discipline gap and the achievement gap. The intention of this chapter is to provide you with techniques that support recognizing adherence and lack of adherence to rules and procedures without creating an impediment to learning.

Chapter 2 addressed techniques for establishing classroom rules and procedures. The strategy *recognizing adherence and lack of adherence to rules and procedures* addresses what to do in order to recognize students who are following the rules and procedures as well as those who are not. It involves thinking about logical consequences and consistency. For students who have struggled and possibly may have lost valuable instruction time in the past, the techniques provided in this chapter offer methods of providing reinforcements and consequences without depriving students of valuable classroom instruction. These techniques, when implemented effectively, can keep students in the classroom, therefore enhancing student learning. It is important to remember that when used inappropriately, these techniques can have the entirely opposite effect and be detrimental to learning (Marzano, 2007). The effective or ineffective implementation of reinforcements and consequences has the potential to positively or negatively impact the achievement gap.

Ways to Effectively Implement Recognizing Adherence and Lack of Adherence to Rules and Procedures

At the core of effective classroom management is the fundamental teacher behavior identified as *withitness*, or the skill of being fully aware of everything that is happening around you at all times. Withitness is used to maintain adherence to rules and procedures. There are four general actions that constitute withitness: being proactive, occupying the entire room, noticing potential problems, and using a series of graduated actions.

Being Proactive

- Be mentally prepared before students arrive. Have an idea of what might take place that could potentially impede instruction. What might go astray with specific students, and how will you address potential problems? These insights will likely develop over the course of the school year. You may come to recognize that environment created by the crowds and noise in the cafeteria has an emotional effect on some students or that a specific student who enters your classroom in the afternoon is often frustrated or angry. Mentally preparing for this behavior or change in mood will allow you to handle the situation calmly and rationally by reframing the situation before it even takes place.

- Attempt to be aware of external influences that have the potential to affect student behavior. Imagine a scenario in which a student takes the bus every morning, and on the bus, there are often arguments or even physical altercations, which result in disruption that spreads into the rest of the instructional day. Speaking privately with students to review behavioral expectations for the day will decrease the chances that the disruptions will affect the rest of the learning environment, but if they do, you will be prepared to diffuse situations as necessary.

- Use prearranged cues with students to signal inappropriate behavior. Many students do not intentionally misbehave but simply require a reminder from time to time. When the student sees the privately agreed-on gesture, he or she may then be given the time to reflect on the situation and control the behavior before it escalates. For example, we knew a teacher who wore three rubber bands on her right arm. This teacher had a private agreement with one student that, when she moved a rubber band to her left arm, these graduated actions constituted a warning. The student knew that the rubber bands were a reminder to correct his behavior. The agreement was that when all three rubber bands moved to her left arm, the teacher would take an elevated action.

Occupying the Entire Room

- Visually scan the room, noting behaviors of individuals or groups of students.

- Make eye contact or catch the gaze of each student.

- Move through all quadrants of the room systematically and frequently.

Noticing Potential Problems

- Recognize potential disruptions as quickly as possible, such as:

    - Several students huddled together talking intensely before class

    - One or more students not engaging in class activities

    - Whispering, giggling, or unusual noises heard when the teacher's back is to the class

Using a Series of Graduated Actions

Once a potential problem has been identified, graduated actions may be taken to immediately stop the misbehavior. The key here is to not escalate a situation to a greater level than necessary. Often, only a minor acknowledgment is required to set a situation back on its desired track.

- Look at the suspected students so they know that their behavior has been noticed.

- Move in the direction of the disruption, continuing to teach. Eventually stand immediately next to the students displaying inappropriate behavior.

- If moving closer does not stop the misbehavior, lean in for a private conversation with the students, asking them to stop the inappropriate behavior.

- If the students still do not stop the behavior and reengage in a positive way, stop instruction and confront the behavior publicly. Stay calm and polite, stating the consequences that will be given for the behavior if it is not corrected. Share with the students that the decision is theirs.

Withitness in and of itself is a useful technique to effectively ensure that students follow the rules and procedures. It is also the gateway to additional techniques to effectively recognize adherence and lack of adherence to rules and procedures. These techniques may be used in conjunction with, or following the use of, withitness and fall into the following categories:

- Verbal and nonverbal cues and affirmations

- Tangible recognition

- Home recognition/contingency

- Direct cost

Verbal and Nonverbal Cues and Affirmations

Cues

Verbal cues are comments that remind students that they are not adhering to rules or procedures:

- Speaking softly

- Asking students to stop

- Repeating a rule to a student

Nonverbal cues are subtle gestures that signal inappropriate behavior:

- Shaking head no

- Tapping a desk

Affirmations

Verbal affirmations are comments that acknowledge students are adhering to rules and procedures:

- "Thank you."

- "Great job."

- "That's excellent."

Nonverbal cues are signals that acknowledge students who are adhering to rules and procedures:

- Smiles

- Nods

- Winks

- High fives

Tangible Recognition

Tangible recognition involves concrete rewards. Recognition may include privileges, activities, or items as motivation to continue positive behavior or to stop negative behavior. Rewards such as Fun Friday activities, science experiments, lunch with the teacher, daily recognition forms, or token economies are all examples of recognition activities. For additional examples of tangible recognition, please see figure 3.1. Marzano suggests that this category of techniques can be most easily misused. If such reinforcement is not accompanied by a discussion of the rationale for the recognition, the meaning may be lost. Additionally, recognition should not be used or viewed as bribery for specific behavior (Marzano, Marzano, & Pickering, 2003). The most powerful rewards recognize positive behavior or are removed for negative behavior. Some specific examples include:

- **Token economies.** Students receive a token for appropriate behavior or for the cessation of inappropriate behavior. This appears to be most useful if tokens are awarded for positive behavior and removed for negative behavior.

- **Goal sheets.** Students striving to accomplish a behavior goal write that goal on a sheet of paper. Each time they are recognized as meeting that goal, they receive some type of tangible recognition on the sheet. This motivates them to persist in reaching the set goal.

- **Group recognition/contingency.** These techniques are similar to tangible recognition techniques. They involve some form of recognition for appropriate behavior. Groups of students are targeted, as opposed to individuals. Group contingencies that require every member of the group to meet a behavioral criterion seem to be most effective.

Home Recognition/Contingency

Home contingency involves bringing parents into the management process. Research shows that involving parents as a positive or negative consequence is a powerful intervention. The efficacy of such interventions is supported by data collected from student responses when they were asked about the following rewards and deterrents (Marzano, 2007):

- Phone calls

- Emails

- Notes home

- Certificates

Figure 3.1: Examples of tangible recognition.

Token Economies	$1 $5 $10 $20 $50 $100
Goal Sheets	*A chosen reinforcer is placed here* → I'm working for ☐ ☐ ☐ ☐ ☐ ☐ ☐ ☐ ☐ ☐ ☐ ☐ ☐ ← *Earned tokens are placed into these spaces*

Group Recognition/ Contingency	Day	Rojo	Amarillo	Verde	Morado	Azul
	Monday					
	Tuesday					
	Wednesday					
	Thursday					
	Friday					

Direct Cost

Direct costs are often a result of a student's inability to self-regulate. They are very deliberate consequences that occur once the negative behavior has gone beyond the point where it could be addressed by withitness (Marzano, 2007).

- **Time out:** A student is removed from classroom activities for a specific time frame.

- **Overcorrection:** This entails having a student not only correct his or her own misdeed but also improve the situation for all.

Common Mistakes to Avoid When Recognizing Adherence or Lack of Adherence to Rules and Procedures

Rules and Procedures Are Established Without Consequences

When rules and procedures have no consequences, students do not see them as necessary or important. Providing consequences for rules and procedures demonstrates the importance of the structure in regard to learning. Students must understand that these consequences not only provide structure to the classroom but also benefit their learning. Consequences make it clear that rules and procedures are necessary components of their learning environment.

Consequences Are Communicated Without Enforcement or Consistency

Without consistency or enforcement of rules and procedures, they become less effective as a tool to support learning. If a rule or procedure is put in place, the demonstration of that rule or procedure must consistently be enforced. Lack of enforcement, both positive and negative, will likely result in lack of adherence.

For example, if students have been asked during a certain activity to refrain from calling out, but enforcement of the rule has not been consistent, it may result in a scenario similar to the one below.

"OK, everyone. I have my calling cards, which means that I will be selecting who answers. Sometimes, I'll ask you to turn to your partner and speak, and other times, I'll be calling on students from my cards. Please refrain from calling out so that everyone gets a turn. I want you to think about the fraction one-fourth. Now, imagine a circle that represents one-fourth. How many parts are in the whole circle, and how many parts are shaded?"

Before the teacher has the opportunity to ask peers to turn and talk, one student in the front of the group calls out the answer. The teacher looks at him but does not react.

"That is correct, Larry, but next time, I would really like for others to have a chance to answer the question."

The teacher poses another question, and this time, Maddie calls out the answer. Again, this is handled passively, although the rules have been clearly stated. "Maddie, I appreciate your enthusiasm, and you had the correct answer. I was really hoping that I could pull a card to give others an opportunity."

During her third attempt to ask a question and avoid callouts, Lewis calls out an incorrect answer. "No, Lewis. That is not correct. I have asked you all to not call out, and you have now had several reminders. Lewis, I am going to have to ask you to return to your seat."

Lewis, and the whole class for that matter, is likely confused. On multiple occasions, students called out and did not face consequences; however, when Lewis called out, he did. Because of the inconsistency, it is likely that Lewis is unsure if he has been sent back to his seat for calling out or for providing an incorrect answer.

Consequences and Reinforcements Are Unbalanced

When consequences and reinforcements are not in balance, students see that negative behavior is weighted more heavily than positive. Giving equal weight to positive reinforcement helps students understand what positive behavior looks and sounds like. If students are able to see positive behavior and are acknowledged for it, they are more likely to begin or continue to behave in that manner. Additionally, attention for positive behavior will increase their desire to act accordingly. Marzano (2007) quotes Good and Brophy (2003) to underscore this point: "It is becoming increasingly clear that the effects of reinforcement depend on the nature of the reinforcement used and especially on how it is presented."

Following is an example of a teacher who uses tangible recognition. The same math lesson from above is presented in much the same fashion. Students have been reminded that calling cards will be used or that they will be asked to turn and talk.

"Before we begin, I want to remind you that you have opportunities to earn or lose coins during this activity. OK, everyone. I have my calling cards, which means that I will be selecting who answers. Sometimes, I'll ask you to turn to your partner and speak, and other times, I'll be calling on students from my cards. Please refrain from calling out so that everyone gets a turn. I want you to think about the fraction one-fourth. Now, imagine a circle that represents one-fourth. How many parts are in the whole circle, and how many parts are shaded?"

Before the teacher has the opportunity to ask peers to turn and talk, one student in the front of the class calls out the answer. This time, the teacher does not dismiss the infraction. "That answer is correct, Larry, but I'm disappointed that you called out. You now owe me a coin." Larry hands over a coin. The teacher poses another question, and this time, Maddie calls out the answer. The result of Maddie's callout is much the same as Larry's. She must return a coin to the bank. When the next question is posed, the teacher sees Lewis squirm in his seat, but he does not call out. By sheer coincidence, she pulls his card from the bucket, and he provides an answer. "Great answer, Lewis. You are correct. Thank you for waiting your turn."

No coin is earned, which demonstrates an imbalance between consequences and reinforcements. Students see that negative behavior is recognized but positive is not.

Opportunities to Teach and Reinforce Conative Skills

Interacting Responsibly

The effective implementation of the techniques addressed in this chapter serves to support and reinforce behaviors aligned to responsible interaction. Using these techniques enhances students' abilities to self-regulate and direct their behavior in a way that supports learning and interactions with others.

As the teacher continues to establish rules and procedures, recognizing adherence or lack of adherence to those rules and procedures also supports responsible interaction. Recall the example from the previous chapter. The teammates were asked to add gems to the conversation. The teacher engaged in several techniques to recognize adherence and lack of adherence during this time. She was able to monitor students to see that they were interacting responsibly by counting the number of gems remaining as well as circulating and listening to student conversations.

> "Great job, Thomas. That was a great contribution to the conversation. When Cammie shared her feelings about the interaction between the two main characters, you were able to politely share a different viewpoint while at the same time recognizing her contribution. Don't forget to add a gem to the bucket."

> "Katrina, I noticed you still have a lot of gems in front of you. I want to remind you that everyone is expected to contribute to the discussion. Teammates, please make sure that everyone has an opportunity, and Katrina please share some gems."

At the high school level, once students have learned the rules and proce-dures for interacting in teams, the teacher may direct students' attention to an anchor chart or give a verbal reminder to interact responsibly.

Avoiding Negative Thinking

The strategies discussed in this chapter motivate students to aspire to adhere to rules and procedures. Mindful attention to recognition of adherence and lack of adherence to rules and procedures provides a supportive environ-ment in which behavior management is a positive experience for all students. They will come to understand that rules and procedures exist for the purpose of enhancing their classroom experience, as opposed to catching them in the act of misbehavior.

If the techniques listed in this chapter are used, students will look forward to recognition for following rules and procedures and will also understand the need for recognition of lack of adherence. Regardless of whether adherence or lack of adherence is being recognized, it is up to the teacher to promote positive thinking. This may be easy when students are following the rules and procedures, but it is during the difficult times of lack of adherence to rules and procedures that students benefit from being taught to avoid negative thinking.

One of the techniques listed is sending a note home, or home recognition. If this technique is only used in times of lack of adherence, students may develop a habit of negative thinking. "The only time my parents hear about my behavior is when I misbehave. Can't I do anything right?"

Instead, be sure to send notes on a regular basis, and point out some-thing that the student is also doing well. Even if lack of adherence must be addressed, balancing the communication can foster positive thinking.

> Dear Parent/Guardian,
>
> As the week draws to a close, I would like to share some highlights from Brendan's week. Our class participated in many whole-group activities this week, and it was clear that Brendan has been working hard to follow the rules and procedures. He has been using the signals we have discussed when he needs to take a minute, and that has been working very well. I have noticed though that when Brendan is working in small groups or independently, he is still a bit disruptive. I would recommend that Brendan work toward contributing more to the conversations with his team and focus on completing his assignments.

An action that could be taken to help Brendan avoid negative thinking in this situation is to review the note with him, being sure to phrase the review in terms of "a glow and a grow." If the teacher explains that he is proud of Brendan's specific accomplishments (the glow) and anticipates he will do better in the areas in which he needs to improve (the grow), this will be a positive experience for Brendan, even though his parent/guardian is being notified of his lack of adherence.

Examples and Nonexamples of Recognizing Adherence and Lack of Adherence to Rules and Procedures

Elementary Example

In a fourth-grade classroom, the teacher has established a token economy. There have been clear guidelines established for how to earn and how to lose tokens. At the beginning of each week, the teacher reviews the token policy.

"Boys and girls, I would like to remind you how the token system works. There are many chances throughout the day for you to earn tokens."

I can earn a token by:	
TOKEN	Staying on task
TOKEN	Following the rules and procedures
TOKEN	Respecting the feelings and property of others
TOKEN	Following directions in a group task (whole group)
I can lose a token by:	
TOKEN	Not following rules and procedures
TOKEN	Being disrespectful
TOKEN	Not following directions in a group task (whole group)

continued ⟶

She references the chart above, which is posted in the class-room. "You may earn up to one token per lesson or section of time during the day. However, you may lose more than one token in that same time frame, because if you continue to break rules and procedures or continue to be off task, you are causing a disruption to others. Remember, you are saving these tokens so that you can purchase treasures from the trea-sure chest at the end of each quarter!"

At the end of each quarter, students use the tokens earned to purchase items from the classroom treasure chest. The students know that each day starts with the potential to earn several tokens, including any tokens earned in groups. They receive these tokens for following all the rules and procedures on an individual basis. There are also times throughout the day when teams are given a specific task and are informed that they will earn additional tokens for specific behaviors or outcomes.

In this example, three students have not followed one of the general rules of the classroom. One of the general rules is to always walk inside the class-room to ensure safety for all. When it is time to gather supplies, designated students are sent to get the supplies for their groups. Three students choose to race back from the supplies, running with scissors in hand, which puts them and others in danger. The teacher immediately and firmly asks the students to stop running.

"Let's take a moment to discuss the rules. 'Always walk inside the classroom.' Why is this rule important?"

One of the students who had been running with scissors responds that it is to make sure that all students, including themselves, are safe.

> "I must ask the three of you to return a token because you broke a classroom rule. You will have opportunities to earn more tokens today, and hopefully you will remember to follow the rules and procedures."

When asked to return a token, they understand and quickly comply. All other students followed the rules and procedures, so they did not lose tokens. There will be opportunities designated throughout the day for teams to earn additional tokens. They will remember in the future that when they fail to follow a rule or procedure, they will have to turn in a token.

In this example, recognition of adherence and lack of adherence to rules and procedures is balanced and routine. The earning and losing of tokens is predictable and unbiased.

Elementary Nonexample

In the same token economy previously discussed, the three students run with scissors in hand. One of the girls who ran has also had difficulty staying in her seat and has called out several times during the lesson. When she arrives to her seat, the teacher asks her to return a token.

> "I noticed that you were running with scissors. One of our classroom rules is 'Always walk inside the classroom.' I think you know that this means that you will have to lose a token."

The student has not had to turn in a token for speaking out of turn, wandering the classroom, or not following several other rules and procedures during the course of the same day. The teacher then turns her attention to the other two students who had also been running.

"I am disappointed that you broke the rules. I should take a token from each of you. I haven't had to speak with you yet today, so I will let you off with a warning. However, since the rest of the class did not break the rules, they will all earn one extra token, and you will not."

In this example, the token economy is unbalanced and unpredictable for students. They are unable to gauge the consequences for their actions. Only one student who broke the rules receives a consequence, while the others are let off with a warning. The entire class then earns tokens, even those who were not fetching materials. The one student who does have a token taken away had no way of predicting that this infraction would cause this consequence because she had broken the rules earlier in the day and had not been required to return a token. Consequences have been inconsistent, and she does not understand why this infraction is deemed worthy of losing a token but other actions were not. Additionally, her peers who also ran are allowed to keep their tokens. This token economy is not effective because it is unpredictable and unbalanced.

Secondary Example

In a classroom full of seniors, the teacher notices a group in the back. They are whispering and chuckling, causing a slight distraction during the lesson. In order to avoid interrupting the lesson, the teacher simply makes eye contact with the students to let them know she sees the behavior. For a short time, the behavior stops.

Later in the lesson, the same group of students begins their conversation again, this time causing students to turn in their direction. Continuing with the lesson, the teacher moves closer to the group. This proximity is intended to stop the behavior without stopping instruction. Since eye contact did not fully send the message, this is the next step of graduated action.

When the students once again become a disruption, the teacher briefly stops talking and addresses the group.

> "I have been watching this take place for a short time. You may not be aware, but your discussion is distracting to others in the class and is taking attention from the lesson. If you choose to continue this behavior, your group will be split up and you will have to complete the assignment on your own."

With the students aware of the consequences, class continues without further interruption. It is likely that anywhere in this scenario the behavior may have been stopped. Quite often, it only takes simple eye contact to let students know that they have your attention and likely the attention of others. If effective relationships have been established, as we will address in chapter 6, the likelihood increases that such simple actions will stop the behavior.

Secondary Nonexample

In the same classroom, students disrupt the class with discussion and laughter. Instead of attempting to rectify the situation with little disruption, the teacher calls out the name of one student in the group. The attention of the class is drawn to the disruptive group. Everyone is taken off task. When the lesson continues, so does the conversation. This time, the teacher addresses the entire group, asking them, in a raised voice, to please stop talking. She tells them that they are disrupting the entire class and they are likely to face severe consequences. When the conversation once again continues, the teacher gets angry and yells at the students. The entire class is again taken off task. This time, the teacher sends the students to the office. She must take time to write passes and an explanation of events to inform administration. She is angry and sends the students to the office, reminding them as they leave the room that they have now taken time away from instruction.

This is an extreme example of what might happen when graduated actions are not used effectively. The result is that the teacher loses her patience and composure, the class loses instructional time, and the students who were talking miss the entire lesson. The intention of graduated actions is to stop this behavior before it becomes a great distraction, not to escalate the situation.

Monitoring for the Desired Result of Recognizing Adherence and Lack of Adherence to Rules and Procedures

If implemented effectively, the result of recognizing adherence and lack of adherence to rules and procedures is that students are following said rules and procedures. The following techniques can help you determine if students are following rules and procedures.

Recognizing Adherence

Acknowledge students who demonstrate appropriate behavior to ensure continued adherence. This calls for constant monitoring of adherence and consistent acknowledgment. Consider some of the following phrases:

- [Student Name], I really like how you _____. Thank you for following the rules.

- [Student Name], I noticed that you _____. Thank you.

- [Group Name] followed the rules by _____.

Observe behavior after tangible recognition has occurred to verify that adherence to rules and procedures persists. It is important to note if the behavior continues after receiving the recognition to determine if further steps or recognition is required.

Determine if students are continuing to follow rules and procedures after notes home. For some, notes home are a powerful acknowledgment, while others will not be impacted. Monitoring for this consistency in behavior will help determine the effectiveness of this technique.

Recognizing Lack of Adherence

Provide reminder comments to students misbehaving or not following rules and procedures. Continue to circulate and ensure that no further misconduct continues. Being aware of how feedback impacts students will help shape next steps and forms of recognition.

After time-out, observe student(s) to see if time away corrected the misbehavior. This technique is not always effective, so it is important to monitor the behavior once the action has been taken. Asking yourself the following questions may guide you in determining the effectiveness of this technique:

- Is the behavior increasing or decreasing? This will help determine if the time-out is possibly having an opposite effect than anticipated. If the behavior is increasing, continue asking questions.

- Does the consequence appear to be a deterrent? It is sometimes assumed that being removed from an activity is a negative consequence for all students. There may be many reasons why a student might actually want to be removed from the class or from a specific lesson. Continue asking questions.

- When is the lack of adherence taking place? Is it sporadic, or is it during certain parts of the day? If the behavior is occurring during the same part of a lesson or day, dig a little deeper.

- Is the student struggling academically? Often a student will act out because it detracts from the fact that he or she is struggling with the content. Removing a student from that situation may actually be detrimental.

Please see the proficiency scale in figure 3.2 to determine your level of proficiency within this strategy.

Figure 3.2: Student proficiency scale for recognizing adherence and lack of adherence to rules and procedures. The proficiency scale identifies phases of implementation regarding the strategy. The "Desired Result" articulates the desired outcome of using the strategy, while "Emerging" and "Fundamental" represent a developmental progression in its use.

Condition	Emerging	Fundamental	Desired Result
Recognizing adherence and lack of adherence to rules and procedures	Establish rules and procedures and communicate them to students.	Plan and implement techniques for recognizing adherence to rules and procedures. Plan and implement techniques for recognizing lack of adherence to rules and procedures.	The desired result of recognizing adherence and lack of adherence to rules and procedures is students follow the rules and procedures.

Scaffold and Extend to Meet Student Needs

Adjustments in instruction may be required to ensure that students are following rules and procedures. These adaptations are dependent on the technique being implemented and should provide the support, scaffolding, or extensions students may need to reach the desired result.

Scaffolding

- Recognize students who may not be affected by affirmations and provide meaningful alternatives.

- Provide graphic representation to show what is required for tangible recognition.

- Have positive notes translated so that they can be understood by families.

- Provide verbal and nonverbal support.

Extending

- Students identify ways to recognize positive contributions.

- Students explain why tangible recognition motivates them.

- Personally visit students' homes.

- Students describe consequences.

- Students make suggestions for overcorrection.

Chapter 4

USING ENGAGEMENT STRATEGIES WHEN STUDENTS ARE NOT ENGAGED

The first two conditions for rigor in this guide focused on establishing rules and procedures and applying consequences when students do not follow the rules. It is often assumed that if students are following the rules and procedures, or being compliant, they are engaged. Engagement can be defined as a high degree of on-task behavior (Fredricks et al., 2004) with tasks that are:

- Appropriately difficult—not so easy as to be boring and not too difficult as to be impossible

- Academically demanding—students will need to exert a certain level of effort to accomplish them

- Worthwhile—students will acquire new skills and knowledge that are essential to succeed in more cognitively demanding tasks

Certainly, engagement includes on-task behavior, but true engagement requires students to be actively and successfully engaged in learning. Instead of simply following directions and going through the motions, students should be immersed in the content of the lesson and actively participating in their learning. Cognitive engagement is an essential condition for rigor; in other words, student engagement is a prerequisite to student learning.

Engaging students at the outset requires a well-crafted lesson that anticipates where some students may lose focus and specifically accounts for students who consistently have difficulties staying on task. Keeping students engaged calls for a set of teacher behaviors that must be enacted in the moment. The moment students begin to drift away for any reason, teachers should be ready to shift gears and bring them back to attention.

You can probably predict in advance which students in your class may have problems engaging and intentionally plan appropriate techniques for those students. But you can't predict everything. Thus, it's important to fill your teaching toolbox with strategies for in-the-moment engagement to reengage students as quickly as possible. Such quick response requires a lot of practice using engagement strategies so they become automatic when needed. Think of it like learning to drive a car. First, you may have read about or studied the basics of driving. Then, you practiced during the permit phase, with an experienced driver to coach you. In these early phases, you likely lacked the automaticity, accuracy, and withitness to scan the environment for potential problems while at the same time steering, braking, and signaling. It may feel similarly cumbersome when you first attempt to manage instructional flow by changing up the variety and momentum of the lesson while simultaneously selecting an attention-getting move from your repertoire. But with time, patience, and persistence, you can manage to master these strategies to use when you need them.

A lack of engagement that persists from lesson to lesson, or class to class, over time makes student academic success less likely. Students who don't adhere to rules and procedures may become progressively disengaged and sometimes detached from learning in general. On the other hand, students may seem persistently noncompliant when, in fact, they are not cognitively engaged in the learning. Teachers should monitor for both compliance and cognitive engagement. As we noted above, student engagement is a prerequisite to student learning.

Consider the examples and nonexamples of student engagement shown in table 4.1.

Ways to Effectively Implement Using Engagement Strategies When Students Are Not Engaged

There are two categories of students who become disengaged: (1) those who are *consistently* disengaged for a variety of reasons and (2) those who are *momentarily* disengaged. Engaging students who are momentarily off task

Table 4.1: Examples and Nonexamples of Cognitive Engagement

Students Are Cognitively Engaged When They Are . . .	Students Are Not Cognitively Engaged When They Are . . .
Reading text at their independent reading levels for a specific purpose	Quietly watching what others are doing, either in the whole class or as part of a small group
Speaking to a partner, as a participating member of a small group, or to the whole class as part of a class discussion	Pretending to be engaged when the task is too difficult for them
Writing a response, either on paper or a whiteboard	Passively listening or giving an impressive imitation of listening
Signaling a response to a question with a physical gesture or a response card	Waiting for a turn during round-robin reading of the textbook
Performing as part of a readers theater	Doing busy or mindless seatwork
Thinking about an answer and then thinking aloud about how they arrived at the answer	Wasting time quietly by daydreaming or sleeping
Practicing discrete skills or rehearsing content in a well-designed academic procedure	Staring at the printed page and pretending to read text that is too difficult for them to understand
Coding text with sticky flags during silent reading to indicate places where they have a question for the author	Doing a word search containing the spelling words of the week
Developing a graphic organizer as the teacher works with the class	Listening to the teacher talk for more than ten minutes without any opportunities to process (or respond)

Source: Adapted with permission from McEwan, 2012.

in the context of a well-planned and effectively taught lesson simply requires some in-the-moment action to reengage them. But students who are consistently disengaged, for whatever reason, require more serious engagement interventions. Knowing there are many reasons why students may not be engaged, teachers should strive to understand the cause of the struggle and choose the correct technique to implement. One important technique to reengage students is to teach them four questions that help explain engagement: How do I feel? Am I interested? Is this important? and Can I do this? (Marzano, 2012).

How Do I Feel?

Students need to feel emotionally safe as well as physically healthy to be fully engaged in any activity. The way students feel has the potential to affect the energy level of the entire classroom. Students' perceptions of acceptance by their peers and teacher play a role in their engagement in the classroom environment. As discussed in chapter 3, a balanced combination of positive and negative consequences should be used to reinforce proper behavior. Ultimately, if students experience a greater volume and frequency of negative consequences, they may become withdrawn and disengaged.

Health and nutrition may also play a role in how students feel. Overall, students who lack exercise, who have undiagnosed illnesses, who are improperly prescribed medications, or who are not provided appropriate interventions are at risk of disengaging. Nutrition is a contributing factor in how students feel. Consuming foods low in nutrition negatively affects cognitive processing, which can affect engagement and, moreover, academic achievement (Jensen, 2009). Jensen (2009) concludes that physical, mental, and emotional health supports engagement and learning, and the existence of health-related factors has a significant effect on cognition and also behaviors.

Other factors, aside from health and nutrition, tend to impact how students feel physically and emotionally. The level of excitement and activity in a classroom influences students' emotions. Being seated for long periods of time slows blood circulation and oxygen going to the brain and decreases energy levels, which can negatively affect engagement (Sousa, 2011). Boredom and fatigue will likely have negative impacts on how students engage, as well.

Am I Interested?

Student interests play an integral role in engagement. Typically, if students are interested in a concept, cognitive engagement is high. The goal of the classroom teacher is to not only teach content but to do so in a way that students connect to the context for learning. Connecting instructional content to students' values and interests can be quite difficult if the classroom teacher knows very little about his or her students. In chapter 5 of this guide, we will discuss the importance of establishing and maintaining effective relationships that not only strengthen the classroom environment but also enhance instruction and feedback.

In 2007, Indiana State University cited a study by Yazzie-Mintz that concluded that given the same context for learning, students reported varying levels of engagement. Thus, the degree of interest students feel in content begins with context. Students may struggle with engagement if the content is presented in a way that does not intrinsically connect with their everyday lives. For example, a reference to Disney World, intended to draw students in and get them excited, may do the opposite if they have never visited Disney World or are unaware of where it is. Teachers need to be sure that students can relate to the presentation. If, because of varying backgrounds, not all students are able to relate to the content in the same way, teachers should provide a context (video, pictures, or stories) before presenting content. Context will level the playing field and allow all students to be equally included.

Is This Important?

Creating relevance and importance for learning is an art. Just as context can promote student interest, context can also help students recognize the importance of the content. But motivating students to value education isn't always easy. Students enter classrooms with different backgrounds that ultimately impact the importance they assign to specific topics or even to education in general. While some students possess a degree of intrinsic motivation that creates engagement, many do not. Students who do not may fail to see the importance of content that does not address their present needs or their expectations of future employment. Students may be wondering, "Is this important to *me*?" and "Why do I need to know this?" Creating an environment in which students believe the content applies to them now and that they will use it in the future is imperative when teaching unmotivated students.

Can I Do This?

Students must be able to understand and visualize their long-term potential. They must recognize that content is important and applicable to them and their future needs. First, students need to feel they are capable of the task at hand. Psychologist Albert Bandura (1991) defines *self-efficacy* as the belief in your ability to succeed in specific situations or accomplish a task. Students who tend to struggle cognitively are more likely to become disengaged due to an internal doubt about their own competence. Though self-efficacy is manufactured internally, a teacher's well-planned use of techniques can alter students' perception of their abilities. As teachers increase the level of complexity and autonomy with respect to instruction, how students answer the question *Can I do this?* plays a major role in how they approach tasks and challenges.

When a teacher recognizes lack of engagement, she should first determine which of the four questions above is negatively affecting student engagement. Marzano (2007) suggests the techniques below to keep students engaged. The critical attribute of these engagement strategies is their relentless emphasis on *content*. Engagement is not about paying attention or staying on task as defined in more traditional ways. Engagement must consistently be in the service of cognitive content; in other words, our purpose as teachers is to engage students in thinking about rigorous content. This focus provides insight into selecting an appropriate strategy when students disengage.

Techniques for Keeping Your Students Engaged

Maintaining student engagement is an important factor to consider when planning for instruction. Planning to use specific techniques during different parts of the lesson will minimize the likelihood that students will disengage. However, it is also helpful to have a repository of in-the-moment activities for these techniques in the event that students do become disengaged. For the following techniques, there are specific activities to plan in advance as well as use in the moment.

Lively Pacing

Keep energy levels high with lively pacing. Keep the activities moving, and avoid interruptions. Pacing is important not only during the lesson but also during transitions.

Techniques to Plan in Advance
- **Parking lot:** To avoid slowing the progress of the lesson, have students write side issues or questions on a sticky note, chart paper, or the board so they may be addressed at a later time.

- **Timely transitions:** Routinely employ logical, decisive, and efficient transitions between activities.

In-the-Moment Technique

- **Modulation:** Speed up or slow down the pace of the lesson to meet the engagement needs of the students.

Physical Movement

Physical activity increases the number of capillaries in the brain and increases the amount of oxygen in the blood. The brain uses this oxygen as fuel. The level of oxygen concentration in the blood correlates with levels of cognitive performance. Even short moderate physical activity has the potential to improve brain function (Sousa, 2011). Although physical activity may not counteract all of the health and nutrition issues students may face, it will contribute greater oxygen intake and higher levels of cognitive engagement.

Techniques to Plan in Advance

- **Body representation:** Ask students to use their bodies to briefly act out important content, terms, or critical aspects of a topic.

- **Vote with your feet (see figure 4.1):** Assign possible responses to questions to different sections of the room. Ask students to move to the location in the room that represents their answer. Then, ask students to explain why they think the response they selected is correct.

Figure 4.1: Vote with your feet. Teacher places posters on the wall, and students stand on the side of the poster with which they agree.

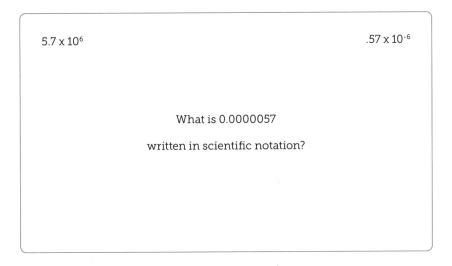

5.7×10^6 $.57 \times 10^{-6}$

What is 0.0000057

written in scientific notation?

In-the-Moment Technique

- **Share and stretch:** Ask students to stand and move to find a partner to share work and ideas, and to increase energy.

Positive Demeanor

A teacher's positive demeanor will demonstrate intensity and enthusiasm for a topic. A positive demeanor will alleviate stress and insecurity in those students who experience more reprimands than positive comments in their home lives.

Techniques to Plan in Advance

- **Personal stories:** Share insight and real-world connections to the content through a personal story to make the information accessible and help students gain a new perspective.

- **Humor:** Integrate funny headlines, silly quotes, amusing questions, cartoons, and intentional errors to integrate humor into the content.

In-the-Moment Technique

- **Verbal and nonverbal signals:** Communicate excitement, interest, passion, and the power of the content through your volume, tone of voice, and emphasis on specific words and phrases. Pause to build anticipation. Smile, gesture, and move around the room while teaching to influence engagement.

Academic Games

Academic games and low-level competition often pique student interest. These games often contain missing information that students want to find, which keeps them interested in the topic.

Techniques to Plan in Advance

- **What is the question:** Place content information into a matrix with content-based categories across the top and progressive point values and levels of difficulty down the side. Divide students into teams and ask teams to select a point value and corresponding content clues. Teams then answer the clue in the form of a question. If the question is complete and correct, award points, and the team wins another turn. If the answer is incorrect or incomplete, the opposing team has the opportunity to provide the correct question. For an example, see figure 4.2.

- **Which one doesn't belong:** Create word groups with three or more similar terms and one that is different. Ask students to work independently or in groups to pick out the term that does not belong and write down why they think it is different.

Figure 4.2: Scoring matrix for "What is the question?".

	Science	Math	Language Arts	Sports/ Arts	General
100					
200					
300					
400					
500					

In-the-Moment Technique

- **Question competitions:** Form teams of equally sized groups, or have students work independently. Pose questions so that students may confer with group members or work individually to record their answers. Give the signal for each student or group to share their answers. The team or student with the most correct answers is acknowledged.

Friendly Controversy

Friendly controversy is another way to capture student interest. Controversy exists when one student's ideas, information, conclusions, theories, or opinions are not compatible with those of another student, and the two seek to reach an agreement. It is not necessary to focus on extremely controversial topics. Begin with something small or relatively inconsequential, such as asking students to share their opinions about something they read in class. Since there are different perspectives, there is still controversy, but it is not so great that it will impede instruction or cause arguments.

Techniques to Plan in Advance

- **Town hall meetings:** Ask students to assume designated roles during a town hall meeting. The town hall format allows students to engage with a complex issue from multiple perspectives. The roles should be based on the people or groups most likely to have a strong opinion about, or be affected by, a new policy or issue. Students argue from their assigned points of view, while the teacher mediates. Debrief after a discussion, and ask students to evaluate their own performances and the discussion as a whole. For an example, see figure 4.3.

Figure 4.3: Matrix for town hall meeting.

Town Hall Meeting		
Topic:	Should the city of Vero Beach enhance the local infrastructure to support tourism or protect conservation areas for their ecological or cultural value?	
Moderator:	Mr. Crespo (Teacher)	
Speaker 1 (for enhancements):		
Speaker 2 (against):		
Speaker 3 (small business owner):		
Speaker 4 (ecologist):		

- **Class vote:** Introduce key points of various positions on an issue, problem, or policy during instruction. Ask students to choose a position and work together to further research the issue and points of view. Ask groups to take turns presenting the facts, opinions, and ideas as they relate to their position on the issue. Students may be swayed by final discussions, and this is the time to switch positions. Finally, ask students to reflect on the thought process that led them to their current perspective on the issue.

In-the-Moment Technique

- **Opposite point of view:** Ask students to defend the opposite point of view from the one with which they agree in order to help them explore the nuances of a particular topic or issue and to reinforce the process of providing evidence to support a claim.

Unusual or Intriguing Information

Presenting unusual information, especially when introducing new content, captures student interest. Unusual information sparks students' curiosity and encourages further engagement in the topic or activity.

Techniques to Plan in Advance

- **Guest speakers:** Invite students to listen to real-world applications of the content being learned as guests share experiences from their careers.

- **Teacher-presented intriguing information:** Share interesting facts or trivia related to the content to capture the attention of students.

In-the-Moment Technique

- **Tweets:** Ask students to share in 140 characters or fewer the most unusual (but factual) information they discovered about a certain topic, adding a hashtag.

Connecting to Students' Lives

Connecting to students' lives creates relevance for both content and task. (See appendix A for resources for connecting with students' lives.)

Technique to Plan in Advance

- **Cognitively complex tasks:** Encourage students to apply knowledge and skills in new situations or real-world applications. When students are challenged to use the information they have learned to solve problems, make decisions, conduct investigations, and create hypotheses about real-world issues, they are more likely to perceive what they are doing as important.

In-the-Moment Technique

- **Providing students with choices:** Providing students with choices about what they engage in or how they can demonstrate their understanding will also keep them engaged. Choice increases intrinsic motivation, effort, task performance, and learning.

Use Clear Learning Targets

To be engaged in learning, students must believe in their own ability to succeed in a specific situation. Such belief is at the heart of self-efficacy. Using clear learning targets provides insight for students to know the direction in which they are working. They will strive for the target, as long as it is provided (for more information on targets, see *Using Learning Targets and Performance Scales,* Moore et al., 2015).

Technique to Plan in Advance

- **Track progress toward the target:** Creating a routine for tracking students' progress to the target allows students to see their growth. Tracking progress toward a target creates an environment in which students will have a positive response to the question "Can I do this?". Personal goals motivate student engagement. The sense of achievement over time supports continued engagement. Using clear expectations and validating small wins acknowledges success, which increases engagement. These tools will help both you and your students focus on the progression of instruction through lessons and units (Moore et al., 2015).

In-the-Moment Techniques

- **Using effective verbal feedback:** Using effective verbal feedback helps students make corrections so they can feel successful and capable. When learning outcomes are articulated in scale format through a progression of learning targets, teachers are able to focus on critical nuances in student work, which enables them to provide focused criterion-referenced feedback. In turn, students are less apt to become detached from the learning or, even worse, unengaged all together.

- **Asking appropriate questions:** Helping students ask appropriate questions when they do not understand and ask questions about feedback is important for developing academic efficacy and, as a result, engagement. This begins with clear expectations. Students must understand not only the learning target but also the evidence of learning. These expectations create the opportunity for students to ask appropriate questions that generate growth and continued engagement.

Common Mistakes to Avoid When Using Engagement Strategies When Students Are Not Engaged

Failure to Recognize When Students Are Not Engaged

Without cognitive engagement, no learning occurs. In 2006, Reeve concluded, "When engagement is characterized by the full range of on-task behavior, positive emotions, invested cognition, and personal voice, it functions as the engine for learning and development" (as cited in Marzano, 2007, p. 99). Students must be cognitively engaged to learn the content. Often, teachers are burdened by the quick pace of curriculum, so instead of allowing students to engage in the material, they attempt to move along too quickly. A fast pace without time for adequate processing or making connections does not lend itself to engagement. However, it's important to distinguish such a fast pace from the lively pace discussed above. Where a lively pace promotes engagement while allowing time for processing, students may struggle with a pace that is simply too fast and become detached from the learning.

Undoubtedly, it is a difficult task to keep 100 percent of students engaged 100 percent of the time; however, consistent monitoring and use of engagement techniques support a teacher's ability to reengage students as needed. Once students are engaged, the teacher has created a fertile environment for learning to occur.

Using Engagement Techniques That Overshadow Learning

Often, the use of engagement techniques overshadows the desired outcome. As different techniques are employed, students should be able to grasp the purpose of each technique as it pertains to their learning. Always refocus student attention to the expected learning or learning target. For example, if a teacher decides to use a question/answer game to review previously taught concepts, and at some point during the game, the teacher realizes that students are more concerned with winning and losing, the teacher would need to redirect students' focus to the educational value of the academic game rather than the competition.

Opportunities to Teach and Reinforce Conative Skills

Conative skills are essential for developing emotional intelligence to apply in real-world situations.

Cultivating a Growth Mindset and Avoiding Negative Thinking

The first step to self-efficacy is the cultivation of a growth mindset. Students must believe that where they are *now* does not define where they can go. Prolonged or persistent failure may be linked to learned helplessness. Chronic stressors and, in this case, the inability to produce satisfactory work may cause students to give up, a form of learned helplessness (Hiroto & Seligman, 1975). The result of repeated failures may lead students to avoid future challenges, for fear of invoking further feelings of failure. Fear of failure inadvertently causes negative thinking and, in worst cases, a lack of engagement or misbehavior. Helping students believe that their level of ability can increase is crucial.

Imagine for a moment a student struggling with fractions. There should be some level of productive struggle, but when the struggle becomes unproductive, and the student begins to believe that he will not be able to succeed, he may disengage completely. Instead of viewing this as an unwillingness to participate, the teacher can view it as an opportunity to teach a growth mindset and help the student learn to avoid negative thinking. For example, students are creating models in science class. The teacher notices that some of the students have become frustrated and are disengaging. A few have even stopped working altogether. There are enough students in the class who have accomplished the task that she decides to use an engagement strategy to reengage the students.

"OK, everyone! Here's what I'd like to see next. I want you to turn to a partner and compare your models. No one is right, and no one is wrong. Partner 1, I want you to go first. Explain your model to your partner and then share why you created it the way you did. Partner 2, I'd like for you to then do the same. When both partners have shared, take the opportunity to make any changes to your models based on any new thinking you have heard."

Interacting Responsibly

Engagement strategies that require students to work together provide a unique opportunity to guide students to interacting responsibly. When students work independently, there are very few moments in which students have this chance. Like the benefits of all conative skills, the benefits of interacting responsibly reverberate far outside the classroom. Students who have learned to interact responsibly are more likely to adhere to rules and procedures in the classroom and will likely carry these skills into college, career, and the rest of their lives.

> "As you compare your models, keep in mind that you have all worked hard. This activity requires you to share your thoughts about your own model. If you have a comment about your partner's work, please keep in mind that he or she has worked just as hard as you have. If, as partners, you disagree about something, remain respectful and use the respectful disagreement sentence starters we have practiced." (See template for ways to respectfully disagree in appendix A.)

Examples and Nonexamples of Using Engagement Strategies When Students Are Not Engaged

Elementary Example

In this example, a third-grade class has been working on making predictions. The teacher starts by placing the students into groups and then provides the directions.

> "Class, today we will be working on making predictions."
>
> In groups, students are asked to discuss the most recently read chapter of a book and predict what will happen next.

continued →

> "After you have discussed the chapter, I want each of you to individually predict what will happen next in the story."
>
> Although they are discussing their predictions with the group, each student is responsible for his or her own product. The requirement for this product is to share a prediction and provide evidence or reasoning to support the claim.
>
> "I want you all to use evidence from the current chapter to come up with what might happen. Once you have come up with a prediction, I want you to decide how you will share your prediction. You can write it out, draw it, or you may even act it out."

Students are then given the freedom to decide how to achieve these directives. They have the choice of acting out their predictions, writing what they think will happen next, or drawing a picture and adding a caption. The choices allow each type of learner to stay engaged with the content in his or her own way.

Elementary Nonexample

In the same third-grade classroom, with the same focus on making predictions, the teacher also asks students to discuss their predictions with a group.

> "Class, today we are going to have a lot of fun making predictions and acting them out."
>
> The teacher decides that it would be fun and interactive to ask students to act out their predictions with the group. While this is fun for many of the students, some are nervous about getting up in front of the class.

continued →

"I would like for everyone to use what is currently happening in the story to come up with what might happen next. Once you have your prediction, I want everyone to share by acting out what they think will happen next in the story."

One student, who has always been shy and self-conscious, refuses to participate. The fear of being in front of the class is greater than his desire to do well on the assignment.

"Johnny, it's time to act out your prediction. Johnny, remember, refusal to share your prediction results in a zero."

He has a strong prediction, with lots of evidence to back it up. But since he will not perform in front of the class, the teacher informs him that he will not get credit for the assignment because he chooses to not participate. Johnny becomes frustrated and decides to not participate in class for the rest of the day.

In this nonexample, the teacher fails to engage all students. By providing choice, the teacher allows each student to demonstrate his or her knowledge and ability in his or her own way. The purpose of the activity is to determine if students can make predictions and use evidence to back them up, not to determine if students can speak in front of the class. Because he is not offered another option, Johnny disengages, even though he has the knowledge and ability to make predictions.

Secondary Example

In a high school history class, the teacher has realized that many of the questions students are asking are not pertinent to the current lesson. In the past, he has struggled with this because he encourages his students to be thinkers and questioners. He wants them to ask questions and relate what they are learning to their current lives and hopes they are intrigued by what they learn.

"All right, students, remember, today our focus is investigating the causes that led to the signing of the Declaration of Independence. I love when you guys ask questions; it tells me that you are all engaged!"

When teachers stop to answer every question that arises during a lesson, the lesson may slow down to the point that necessary content is not covered. Students who do not share the same question or who feel that the question is not applicable to what they are learning are likely to disengage if too much time is spent answering the question.

"As we get deeper into our discussion of the causes leading to the signing of the Declaration of Independence, let's remember to ask questions that specifically relate to our topic. However, in this class, no question is ever a bad question. For those who have questions that aren't directly related, I have something for you."

The teacher in this example has solved the problem by introducing a parking lot. He has designated a bulletin board in the back of the room for this space. It is out of the way and students can get to it without disrupting class. When students want to ask questions not directly related to the topic, they are encouraged to write the questions down on sticky notes and place them in the parking lot.

Student: "Mr. Whitaker, I have a question."

Teacher: "Absolutely, Jada. Is it related to our topic?"

Student: "Well . . ."

Teacher: "No worries. Parking lot!"

If an off-topic question is still asked in class, the teacher simply says, "Parking lot," with a smile, and students know what to do. When students are working independently, the teacher reads the questions and addresses them individually. If there is a question that may benefit the group, he finds an appropriate time to address it with the class.

This strategy allows for the lesson to continue at an appropriate pace without devaluing students' questions.

Secondary Nonexample

The nonexample takes place in a similar setting. Without a procedure in place to handle off-topic or frequent questions, lessons are often slowed or taken off course. Either the goal of the lesson is not achieved or students who are not interested in the extra questions are no longer engaged. Not having a clear procedure in place results in less-effective instruction for all.

Monitoring for the Desired Result of Using Engagement Strategies When Students Are Not Engaged

Monitoring for this strategy requires teachers to determine if students are actively engaged in learning. Are students participating and interacting responsibly while connecting with the content? The following techniques assist in monitoring this strategy:

- Watch and intermingle as students prepare written answers to questions during academic games to determine if they are engaged.

- Circulate and listen to student conversations during academic games.

- Scan the room to ensure engagement is preserved.

- Study student actions during transitions.

Please see the proficiency scale in figure 4.4 (page 74) to determine your level of proficiency within this strategy.

Figure 4.4: Student proficiency scale for engagement. The proficiency scale identifies phases of implementation regarding the strategy. The "Desired Result" articulates the desired outcome of using the strategy, while "Emerging" and "Fundamental" represent a developmental progression in its use.

Condition	Emerging	Fundamental	Desired Result
Using engagement strategies when students are not engaged	Students are aware of their inabilities to stay engaged and recognize when the teacher is making attempts to reengage them.	Students engage in learning most of the time. When students become disengaged, they reengage when an engagement strategy is used.	Students are consistently cognitively engaged in learning. If students become disengaged, they promptly reengage without prompting from the teacher.

Scaffold and Extend to Meet Student Needs

To reach the desired result of the strategy, you may need to make adjustments in instruction. These adjustments, or adaptations, depend on the technique you are implementing and should provide extra support or extension for students to reach the desired result.

Scaffolding

- Allow students to confer with others when working independently.

- Provide visual cues.

- Explain the concept of being overwhelmed or bored, and establish signals.

- Create a signal or gesture to be used each time critical content or big ideas are being presented.

- Inform students of upcoming content.

Extending

- Students keep a list of questions during a lesson and use them for an impromptu game.

- Ask students to identify and correct partners' errors.

- Ask students to look for patterns in the pace of a lesson.

- Ask students to provide feedback on the teacher's use of verbal and nonverbal cues.

- Ask students to identify how learning the content has affected their lives.

Chapter 5

ESTABLISHING AND MAINTAINING EFFECTIVE RELATIONSHIPS

In *The Art and Science of Teaching*, Marzano (2007) notes, "The one factor that surfaced as the single most influential component of an effective school is the individual teachers within that school" (p. 1). Above any other factor, individual teachers have the strongest impact, both positive and negative, on student achievement. Teachers are capable of both promoting academic success and stifling it. Mouton et al. (1996) found, for example, that low-achieving high school students often feel removed or alienated from their schools. These students report believing that no one cares and that teachers don't like them. Jensen (2009) has posited that these feelings of alienation cause many students to give up on academics altogether. Marzano (2007) has written that "arguably the quality of the relationship teachers have with students is the keystone of effective management and perhaps the entirety of teaching" (p. 149).

In the work of Mouton et al. (1996), students are referred to as "low-attached." One way the authors explain or define *attachment to school* is having a sense of belonging. The sense of alienation that low-achieving students felt was demonstrated through student withdrawal from school activities, discipline and attendance issues, negative overall attitudes about school, and in many cases, school dropout. When students identified as high-risk for school failure but who were ultimately successful were asked about the contributing factors to their success, they cited relationships with teachers, counselors, principals, and peers. Additionally, statements recorded from students who did not succeed included "Teachers make me feel dumb," "Teachers don't want me to do well," and "Teachers treat me worse than other students" (Mouton et al., 1996).

Based on this research, we can surmise that the relationships teachers build with their students have the power to foster success or failure. Every student who walks through a classroom door will be impacted by his or her relationship with the teacher. The significance and gravity of fostering and maintaining effective teacher-student relationships could not be clearer.

Two essential components foster and maintain effective teacher-student relationships: (1) guidance and control and (2) cooperation and concern (Marzano, 2007). To establish this fourth condition of rigor, teachers may have to adopt a slightly different role or mindset than that for previous conditions. Establishing and maintaining effective relationships necessitates that teachers reflect on their personal approach to ensure an adequate balance between the two components. Often, teachers begin their careers strong in the area of cooperation and concern (advocacy) and gradually move to become stronger in the area of guidance and control (dominance) (Marzano, 2007). For examples of each of these components, see figure 5.1.

Let's first examine guidance and control. Through this component, teachers communicate to students that the teacher is responsible for providing guidance and control and a level of dominance, both behaviorally and academically. Wubbels and colleagues (Wubbels, Brekelmans, van Tartwijk, & Admiral, 1999; Wubbels & Levy, 1993) define dominance in this context as the teacher's ability to provide clear purpose and strong guidance regarding both academics and student behavior.

Marzano and Marzano (2003) have noted that when asked about their preferences for teacher behavior, students often prefer this type of teacher-student interaction. When guidance and control are implemented effectively, teachers need to address two components: direction in terms of learning outcomes and behavioral expectations (Marzano, 2007). For example, learning targets within a performance scale serve as the guidance system for the learning journey. A calculated and precise recognition of adherence or lack of adherence to rules and procedures is the system for the behavioral expectations.

The second component of establishing and maintaining effective relationships, cooperation and concern, contends that both teacher and students are working together for the betterment of both parties. Both teachers and students communicate and perceive a sense of teamwork. The teacher strives to ensure that students sense that their teacher is concerned for the well-being of the entire class as well as each student individually (Marzano, 2007).

Figure 5.1: Characteristics of each component.

Guidance and Control	• Clarity of purpose and strong guidance
	
	    ○ Academic guidance
	
	        • Provide strong direction of academic content.
	
	        • Communicate learning goals.
	
	        • Track and celebrate student progress.
	
	    ○ Behavioral guidance
	
	        • Establish and maintain classroom rules and procedures.
	
	        • Acknowledge adherence and lack of adherence to rules and procedures.

Cooperation and Concern	• Emotional objectivity
	
	    ○ Avoidance of emotional ups and downs in the classroom
	
	    ○ Avoidance of taking the actions of students personally
	
	• Demonstration of concern for students
	
	• A sense of community in the classroom

Source: Marzano, 2007.

Using a balance of guidance and control (dominance) and cooperation and concern (advocacy), teachers are able to create purpose both academically and behaviorally while supporting the notion that they have a personal stake in the success and well-being of their students.

In many cases, conflicts between students and teachers indicate an interpersonal problem rather than a punishable infraction. The causes of many classroom behaviors labeled and punished as rule infractions are in fact problems of students and teachers who have not yet established strong relationships. This often occurs because the teacher has, regardless of intention, developed an "us and them" mentality when relating to students (Marzano, 2007).

Ways to Effectively Implement Establishing and Maintaining Effective Relationships

In the following pages, we will look at three categories of techniques for establishing and maintaining effective relationships: understanding students' interests and backgrounds, displaying objectivity and control, and using verbal and nonverbal behaviors to indicate affection. These techniques, when used effectively, help to ensure that students feel like part of the classroom community (Marzano, 2012).

Techniques for Understanding Students' Interests and Backgrounds

- **Opinion questionnaires:** Distribute opinion polls that ask students about their perspectives on classroom content.

- **Teacher-student conferences:** Provide opportunities for one-on-one conferences to ask probing questions to help better understand students' interests, perspectives, and experiences.

- **Six-word autobiographies:** Ask students to write an autobiography in exactly six words. Then, lead a discussion in which students share and explain their autobiographies.

- **Quotes:** Ask students to collect and share quotes that describe their personalities and interests and show personal connections to the content. They may be relayed in many different forms.

  - Tweet: In fewer than 140 characters, describe your personality or interests.

  - Write a brief newspaper article about yourself—an accomplishment you are most proud of.

  - Create an author bio to place at the beginning of an important piece of work.

- **Facebook posts:** Place a content topic post on the wall, providing the opportunity for students to add comments to the thread as they relate to the original post.

Techniques for Displaying Objectivity and Control

- **Interpreting communication styles:** Understand how various communication styles affect communication and emotional reactions. This understanding helps prevent teachers from taking student behavior personally.

Figure 5.2: Five communication styles.

Five Communication Styles
The Assertive Connector
Is not engaged in other tasks.
Faces speaker and uses consistent eye contact.
Mirrors the speaker's emotions; for example, if the speaker is sad, the listener's face reflects sadness.
Spends equal time speaking and listening.
Expresses emotions appropriately.
Uses body language that matches the emotion being communicated.
Asks for clarification or elaboration; asks questions respectfully.
Deliberately attempts to fully understand the content and the emotions being expressed by the other person.
Repeats what was said to ensure understanding (for instance, "What I heard you say is. . .").
Can express agreement, disagreement, or neutrality.
Engages in conversation in a win-win manner with the intention to connect with the other person and resolve any issues.
Sends this meta-message: "I value our relationship and what you have to say."
The Apathetic Avoider
Ignores the other person's presence or attempt to speak.
Pauses too long before replying, barely replies, or does not reply.
Interrupts or interjects own thoughts while the other person is speaking.
Is distracted while working or talking to the other person; displays distraction through body movements, such as tapping.
Conveys being apathetic, detached, or distracted.

continued →

Talks while the other person is talking or talks for long periods without listening.

Does not mirror the other person, uses body language that is inconsistent with what is being said by either person.

Turns away, looks away, or walks away.

Avoids relationship with the other person.

May experience considerable anxiety when attempting to connect with another person.

Sends this meta-message: "I don't want much of a relationship with you and will put minimal effort into it."

The Junior Therapist

Takes a one-up position—assumes that he or she is better able to speak for someone than that person is.

Talks for the other person, telling the other how he or she feels, thinks, and acts.

Tells the other person how he or she should feel, think, and act.

Tends to talk about the other person rather than about himself or herself.

Criticizes the other person for his or her feelings, thoughts, and actions.

Decides how the other person is or should be, then responds only when the person acts in accordance with that perception.

Tells the other person that the advice being given is for the other person's own good.

Uses prior knowledge of the person's history in an amateur way, "analyzing" why the person feels, thinks, or acts in a particular way that benefits the speaker's point of view.

Uses knowledge about the other person to distort that person's point of view, often to enhance his or her own argument in hopes of "winning" the conversation.

Sends this meta-message: "I know you better than you know yourself. I know you better than I know myself."

The Bulldozer

Focuses on own topic and ignores topics brought up by the other person.

Switches from the other person's topic to a topic of his or her own liking; dominates the conversation.

Repeats the same thing many times over.

May speak in a louder-than-necessary voice, shout, or scream.

Engages in aggressive behavior—attacks, blames, criticizes, belittles, intimidates, invalidates, or mocks the other.

May engage in name calling, using sarcasm, or using a condescending tone in an attempt to harm the other person's self-esteem or point of view, and ultimately, to "win" the conversation, making the other "lose."

Attempts to make the other person appear incompetent, inferior, unintelligent, or childish, and implies that the other person generally lacks the positive qualities that the bulldozer believes he or she has.

May use violence or intimidation to suggest violence.

Sends this meta-message: "I will do whatever it takes to get my way."

The Hider

Speaks too softly for the listener to hear.

Uses incomplete, incongruent, unclear, paradoxical, or ambiguous sentences; may talk a lot but say little.

Uses contradictory adverbs, over-qualification, or words that indicate unclear status, such as "maybe, sort of."

Pulls away from listener; body language conveys fearfulness or confusion.

Doesn't respond to personal questions or says very little; "hides out" in a group.

Body language, voice tone, and message are not congruent because the person frequently is trying to pretend that he or she is not hiding.

Appears afraid of being heard, criticized, or confronted; assumes that he or she will "lose" the conversation and would rather leave and not continue talking.

Sends this meta-message: "I am afraid of you and don't want you to know about me."

Source: Marzano et al., 2005.

- **Active listening and speaking:** Interact with students in a calm and controlled manner. Focus on what the student is saying and try to understand his or her viewpoint. Remain neutral in body posture, gestures, and facial expressions, but acknowledge that the student was heard by summarizing his or her statement.

- **Self-reflection:** Reflect daily on your own consistency in enforcing positive and negative consequences to determine if there is a balance between the two. If not, further reflection is necessary to better exhibit consistent objectivity in the future.

In table 5.1, you will find some examples of reflection questions to consider regarding these specific behaviors.

Table 5.1: Reflection Questions for Displaying Objectivity and Control

Teacher Reflection Question	If No . . .	Suggested Actions (Marzano, 2007)
Did I react the same way for similar infractions of the rules or procedures?	How can I better prepare myself to react in a consistent manner? Which behavior or reaction was most effective in achieving the desired result?	Track or mentally review the day, noting adherence or lack of adherence to rules and procedures. Plan a specific acknowledgment for each.
Do I show disruptive students that although their behavior is unfavorable, I still view them as productive members of the class? Have I positively motivated my students to adhere to the rules and procedures?	How might I improve my relationship with disruptive students?	Recognize that emotions are natural, but monitor those thoughts and emotions throughout the day. Maintain a cool exterior by avoiding pointing a finger, raising your voice, glaring, or ridiculing. Speak directly and calmly. Maintain appropriate distance. Maintain a neutral facial expression.
Did I help my students understand or describe their offending behavior?	How might I further assist my students in understanding their behavior?	Specifically point out the actions of the student. Comment on behavior as opposed to perceived motives for behavior.

Techniques for Using Verbal and Nonverbal Behaviors to Indicate Affection

- **Scheduled interaction:** Select a few students each day to seek out and talk to—in class, in the lunchroom, between classes, or before or after school. It is helpful to create a schedule to ensure regular interaction with each student.

- **Attend student functions:** Show interest in students by attending students' after-school activities. Let students know you plan to attend, and try to connect with the students at the function.

- **Assign student roles:** Assign rotating roles to specific tasks such as distributing materials, taking care of the class pet, or collecting assignments. This simple process indicates affection.

- **Humor:** Use playful banter, jokes, or self-directed humor to create an enjoyable, positive learning environment. Initiate days like Joke Friday, Funny Hat Day, or Mismatched Sock Day to create a warm, fun climate in the classroom. Reduce the stress of test taking by adding humorous items to tests or even homework and other assignments. Ask students to incorporate humor into their writing when possible or keep a quote board to post funny quotes and invite students to do the same (Elias, 2015).

Common Mistakes to Avoid When Establishing and Maintaining Effective Relationships

Singling Students Out in Front of the Class

Regardless of how a student makes you feel, it is important to always remain levelheaded. Singling students out in front of the class puts them in the spotlight. Students react differently to being singled out. Some thrive on it and act out with the intention of being singled out, which is highly unproductive. Others are embarrassed. They feel ashamed and angry, which is likely to hinder further maintenance of an effective relationship with that student or even escalate behaviors.

Most teachers have experienced the student who intentionally misbehaves, looks to see if the behavior is being noticed, and continues until he or she is corrected in front of an audience. Then there are those students who are so embarrassed by being singled out that they are hesitant to participate in regular classroom activities for fear of being singled out again. In an even worse circumstance, a student will become angry, which is at minimum disruptive to the class and may even escalate to a level that puts others in danger.

Raising Your Voice or Losing Your Temper

For the same reason, raising your voice or losing your temper will lessen the likelihood of an effective relationship. The expression of anger is likely to invoke anger or fear, diminishing the effectiveness of the relationship. This type of behavior is also likely unpredictable. When unable to predict the behavior of their teacher, students may be hesitant to form a relationship with him or her.

When a teacher loses his or her temper, it usually surprises students. It's common for students to react with fear, because the situation is uncertain. Or, students may become defensive or confused.

Teachers who consistently react with a levelheaded approach will establish a foundation for creating trusting relationships with students.

Opportunities to Teach and Reinforce Conative Skills

Becoming Aware of the Power of Interpretation

Human beings interpret their surroundings based on their own history and knowledge. The difficulty is that most people are unaware that their perceptions and interpretations do not always reflect reality (Marzano et al., 2013). For this reason, educators need to become aware of their own interpretations and how those interpretations impact their interactions with students and peers. A student tapping his pencil after already being asked to stop, for example, may not even be aware that he is still tapping. But a teacher may interpret this as intentional misbehavior and blatant disregard for the rules. The teacher may become agitated or deliver a consequence that will only serve to confuse the student. The teacher should take a quick inner inventory of her interpretations and perceptions before reacting. Explicitly modeling these thoughts and behaviors for students demonstrates a key conative skill that students must also develop.

> "Ethan, I've asked you to stop tapping three times, and I notice that it is still happening. My first instinct is to assume that this is intentional and take away your writing utensil. But I think it's also possible that this is an unconscious habit you have developed. Could you please place your pencil inside your desk to avoid it being so accessible?"

Often, students have not readily developed this skill at home, but when the awareness is modeled ("My first instinct is to assume . . . but it's also possible . . .") and intentionally practiced, it will become the norm in the classroom. When this type of behavior and thinking becomes the norm, teacher-student and peer relationships will become more accepting and effective.

Avoiding Negative Thinking

One way teachers can avoid negative thinking is by displaying objectivity and control. Both teachers and students should practice developing their awareness of interpretations, perceptions, perspectives, and actions related to thoughts. In table 5.2 (page 88), the examples show how our perceptions can be interpreted (or misinterpreted) positively or negatively.

To avoid reactions based on negative thinking, the thinking itself must be addressed. Sometimes, parents unknowingly expose children to stress and negative thinking, causing the children to take on this same distress (Jensen, 2009). Students from these environments will likely be unaware of their negative thoughts. If avoiding negative thinking is not consistently displayed and modeled by the teacher by displaying objectivity and control, it is not likely that students will gain this skill on their own.

Once students are made aware of their thinking, or the situations that create negative thoughts, they can then use specific strategies, such as monitoring their inner dialogues with a focus on positivity and being prepared for situations that may lead to negative thinking. This focus and preparation will help maintain more effective relationships and a positive culture in the classroom and prepare students for college and career.

Table 5.2: Identifying Positive and Negative Interpretations

Develop Awareness Of:	Definition (Merriam-Webster, 2017)	Example	Check Your Thinking
Interpretation	The way something is explained or understood	"The teacher is smiling. She must be happy." "That student is staring out the window. He must not be paying attention."	What might I ask to confirm my belief? What else might be causing that behavior?
Perception	A mental image	"My teacher asked me to revise my work but let everyone else turn theirs in. She must not like what I did."	Might I ask the other person's true intention? How will I do this in a nonconfrontational manner?
Perspective	A particular attitude toward or way of regarding something; a point of view	Teacher: "I know my students can do more. I will push them to extend their thinking." Students: "She's being very hard on us and is expecting so much. She doesn't think the work we did was good enough."	What might another person be feeling or thinking in this situation? How might this feel from a different point of view?
Action	A thing done	Yelling, glaring, smiling, waving, pacing	Are my actions reflective of how I am feeling? Do these behaviors have a positive or negative impact on others?

Handling Controversy and Conflict Resolution

As we noted previously, controversy and conflict are inevitable. When two people with differing beliefs disagree, controversy ensues. Conflict occurs when the goals of one person impede the goals of another. Effective relationships cannot be built or maintained if conflict resolution is not addressed and consistently practiced. Granting opportunities for students to speak about their backgrounds, interests, and beliefs allows both teacher and students to get to know one another. Although controversy and conflict will always exist, approaching them with knowledge and understanding of others helps all involved become capable of handling and resolving them.

Prompts for Students to Handle Conflict

I see it differently because . . .

Is your position that . . .

I hear you saying that . . .

The reason I feel as I do is . . .

I believe . . .

Examples and Nonexamples of Establishing and Maintaining Effective Relationships

Elementary Example

In this example, a second-grade teacher knows how important it is that all of her students feel valued and part of the classroom community. Accordingly, she rotates assigned roles weekly. The roles in the class include materials distribution and collection, class line leader, board wiper, class messenger, and materials inspector. To ensure that she does not unintentionally leave students out, she has designed a predictable and equitable system of rotation.

> "Good morning, everyone. Welcome back from the weekend. I'm excited to hear all about what you did a little later in the day. Right now, we are going to assign our weekly roles. Let's all take a look at the rotation board and see who is up."

A job board (pocket chart) is clearly displayed and easily accessible to students. Each job is listed on the left, and notecards with names of students are to the right, always in the same order. Each week, the name on the top is removed; all of the other names move up one spot, and a new name is added to the bottom.

> "Katie, since you made your way all the way up to materials distribution and collection last week, your name goes to the bottom of the rotation. Susan, you will now take that role. William, you will be our class line leader, and Ayana will become the board wiper. Choi, you have the role of class messenger, and Robert, you are up next to join the rotation as materials inspector. Does anyone have any questions about his or her role this week?"

All students know how to do each role, and they feel as though they are contributing to the class and are respected enough to be given a role. The students often burst with pride when performing their assigned duties.

Elementary Nonexample

In a classroom down the hall from our example class, the teacher has some concerns about assigning roles to certain students. Their behavior makes her fear that they will be unable to perform certain tasks, which results in some students being chosen to fill the limited roles each week, while others are overlooked.

Figure 5.3: Sample job board.

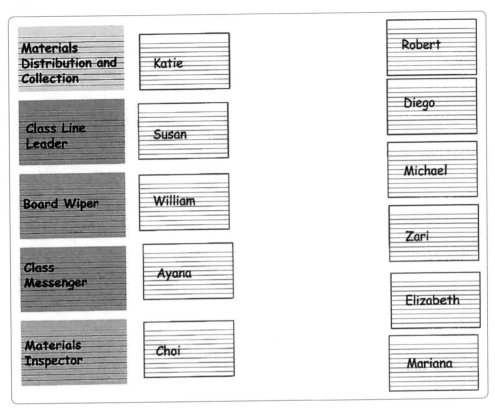

"Good morning, class. Welcome back from the weekend. We should now be ready to focus on class. Let's start by reviewing our assigned roles. Katie, last week you were responsible for materials distribution and collection. You did a great job, so I would like you to remain in that position for another week. Susan, I'll move you back into the rotation on the right. William, you may be class line leader, but if I see you act out, you will lose your job. Mariana has earned the right to be class messenger, so, Choi, I would like to make you an alternate line leader."

Although it is not her intention to exclude certain students from participating, the result is that some of the students who are not often chosen for roles feel alienated and do not believe that they are valued as part of the classroom community. This negative feeling interferes with both their achievement and their behavior.

Secondary Example

This example takes place in a high school algebra class. While reviewing homework from the previous evening, Ms. Forman notices that one student does not have the assignment. The expectation in this class is that homework is completed as practice of a skill previously learned, and it is used only to review before moving forward and building on a concept. Homework is never graded, but students understand that it will be used as part of the lesson and understand the necessity of completing it.

As the review of homework begins, the teacher notices that one student is not participating and does not have his homework on his desk. As students are working, she calmly approaches the student. She keeps her body language, voice, posture, and facial expressions neutral as she listens to him.

> "Jeremy, I notice that you are not participating. Could you please take out your homework so that you can participate in the review?"
>
> "I did my homework. I promise! I left my folder on the table, and I think my brother took it with him to elementary school. It's just stupid homework. It's not like you grade it anyway. Am I in trouble?"

When he is finished, she summarizes his words so that he knows he was heard and then offers a solution.

> "You left your work at home, but it was completed. You are correct; I don't grade the homework, but it is an important part of the lesson today. You are not in trouble. These things happen, and I understand, but I would still like for you to benefit from the review. I'll bet Brian won't mind sharing his homework with you so that you can both review."

The teacher de-escalated a potentially heated situation. Although the student did not bring his homework and even though she may have been internally frustrated by this, she found a way for him to benefit from the activity. The student started out agitated, but by remaining calm and listening to the student, the teacher was able to hear what the issue was, acknowledge his concerns, and find a suitable solution.

Secondary Nonexample

In a similar situation, the teacher listens to the same story. Only this time, instead of showing the student that he has been heard, the teacher outwardly expresses her frustration.

> "Jeremy, I notice that you are not participating. Could you please take out your homework so that you can participate in the review?" "Homework is not optional. You know the expectation and should not have left your work at home. I guess you can sit quietly while everyone else reviews, and you can rejoin the lesson when we move on. Perhaps next time you won't be so careless." "I did my homework. I promise! I left my folder on the table, and I think my brother took it with him to elementary school. It's just stupid homework. It's not like you grade it anyway. Am I in trouble?"

The student hastily piles his notebook on top of his textbook and shoves it into his backpack. With a scowl on his face, which is red from embarrassment and anger, he stares forward. Even when the lesson resumes after the homework review, the student is withdrawn and does not further participate.

This teacher allowed her frustration to affect her relationship with the student. The student does not believe that the teacher has heard what he said. Now, on top of his frustration about not having his work, he is angry, hurt, and frustrated that his teacher did not listen to him. The result is a much less effective teacher-student relationship.

Monitoring for the Desired Result of Establishing and Maintaining Effective Relationships

Monitoring the implementation of this strategy requires determining whether students feel like part of the classroom community. When effective relationships exist, students' rapport and behavior demonstrate a feeling that the teacher accepts and values them.

- Scan responses to opinion questionnaires and ensure that students' perspectives are infused when presenting content. Extrapolate answers from the questionnaires to infuse into lessons. For example, if a lot of the students in the class are interested in cars because a new movie came out about them, use driving speed as a number comparison game or tires as fractional units of a whole. Perhaps a high school teacher has discovered that many of her students watch the same reality show. He or she might use a news article or clip of the show to introduce a topic or begin a conversation.

- Take note of both verbal and nonverbal responses provided by students during teacher-student conferences. This will help to better understand students' desires, hopes, and interests. When discussing areas of improvement, for example, watch the student's face. Does he or she seem eager to make the adaptations or frustrated and overwhelmed at the thought of revision? Ask probing questions to determine what exactly is causing the feelings.

- Circulate and review six-word autobiographies. Ask students to create posters for the autobiographies and note word choice and reflected personalities. The information gathered from this activity will once again serve as a catalyst for delivering relatable lessons.

- Watch students during interactions to verify that reactions and demeanor do not demonstrate personal offense. Whether you are delivering humor or correcting an action, monitor students' reactions to determine their interpretations. If students seem frustrated, annoyed, angered, or otherwise put off by the delivery of information, you should be ready to make adaptations. The intention of each technique discussed in this chapter is to establish and maintain effective relationships, and effective relationships are only possible if interaction does not offend or otherwise antagonize or disturb the students.

- When students are actively speaking and listening, interact with them to confirm tone of voice, body language, and feedback to create an atmosphere of cooperation. Monitoring student tone and body language provides feedback regarding the interaction and the opportunity to make corrections to or clarify intentions during the interaction.

- Observe students in class to determine if their interactions demonstrate that they feel accepted and supported. Some questions you may ask yourself are:

  - Do students seem comfortable approaching me with a question or concern?

  - Do students feel comfortable approaching other students?

  - Are my students eager to participate or apprehensive?

  - Do students willingly interact with one another?

  - Have I observed students offering to help one another?

- While using humor, scan the room looking for students who may not enjoy humor or react negatively to it in the classroom. As mentioned above, if the humor is making students uncomfortable, it is important to change the delivery immediately so that relationships continue to be effective. For example, if a reference to a *Saturday Night Live* skit is used, and students are not familiar with the skit, they may seem bewildered or nonreactive (Wanzer, 2002). If the intention is for this reference to link to lesson content, students will likely be confused as well. Again, recognition and adaptation are key to getting the lesson back on track and maintaining positive relationships with students.

Please see the proficiency scale in figure 5.4 (page 96) to determine your level of proficiency within this strategy.

Figure 5.4: Scale for monitoring progress in establishing and maintaining effective relationships. The proficiency scale identifies phases of implementation regarding the strategy. The "Desired Result" articulates the desired outcome of using the strategy, while "Emerging" and "Fundamental" represent a developmental progression in its use.

Condition	Emerging	Fundamental	Desired Result
Establishing and maintaining effective relationships	Teacher is aware of students' interests and backgrounds, indicates appropriate affection, and behaves in an objective manner.	Teacher fairly and equitably establishes relationships with all students.	The desired result of establishing and maintaining effective relationships is that all students feel like part of the classroom community.

Scaffold and Extend to Meet Student Needs

You may have to adjust instruction to reach every student. The adaptations below depend on which technique you are implementing; they are intended to provide extra support, scaffolding, or extension that students may need to reach the desired result.

Scaffolding

- Allow students to record or verbally share their responses to questionnaires.

- Post graphic representations that clearly explain what is required to earn tangible recognition during teacher-student conferences.

- Share an example of your own six-word autobiography.

- Conference with students who have conflict with you or other students in order to address their needs.

- Ask clarifying questions and use de-escalation techniques to establish an atmosphere of cooperation.

- Solicit compliments about students' accomplishments from other teachers, and share them during scheduled interaction.

- Provide background knowledge to ensure students understand jokes and humor used in the classroom.

Extending

- Ask students to create artwork, musical compositions, or written pieces in response to opinion questionnaires.

- During teacher-student conferences, ask students to identify interests and perspectives they would like to explore in depth.

- Ask students to use belongings and items that help them explain who they are and what is important to them instead of writing a six-word autobiography.

- Ask students to compare their communication style to less effective communication styles.

- Keep track of what was already discussed with students during scheduled interactions in order to follow up on the same topic in future interactions.

- Invite students to share preapproved jokes or funny sayings about content with the class.

Chapter 6

COMMUNICATING HIGH EXPECTATIONS FOR ALL STUDENTS

Most educators, when questioned, sincerely believe they have high expectations for their students. School and district vision and mission statements often emphasize a commitment to high expectations for all students. Creating the final condition for rigor requires teachers to look closely and honestly at personal expectations for their students—which isn't always easy. Saphier and Gower (1997) describe the difficulty:

> Classrooms are dynamic and complex societies with expectations: expectations that teachers have for students, and that students have for teachers and for each other. These expectations explain a good deal of what we see when we visit a classroom—both the good and the bad, the productive and the wasteful. But the expectations themselves cannot be seen. They hang in the air almost like an atmosphere; they exist only between people and comprise a part of their relationship. (p. 47)

In other words, teachers and students both need to strive to make this invisible "atmosphere" of expectations visible. Communicating high expectations for all students is a complex endeavor—it requires all hands on deck, from the superintendent to cafeteria and custodial staff. Operationalizing high expectations for low-expectancy students, however, can be easier said than done. Marzano (2007) notes that expectations often operate unconsciously and influence student learning:

> A teacher's belief about students' chances of success in school influences the teacher's actions with students, which in turn influences student achievement. If the teacher believes stu-

dents can succeed, she tends to behave in ways that help them succeed. If the teacher believes that students cannot succeed, she unwittingly tends to behave in ways that subvert student success. This is perhaps one of the most powerful hidden dynamics of teaching because it is typically an unconscious activity. (p. 162)

Saphier and Gower, along with Marzano, identify this dynamic as unconscious and critical to student success. Even in classrooms where teachers have the best intentions, low-expectancy students may still receive reduced levels of attention compared to high-expectancy students. Marzano concludes that contrasts in the frequency, duration, and type of interaction between teachers and students are often dictated by a teacher's belief about that student's ability to succeed.

As a result, perceptions about the abilities of certain students may already be in place before those students ever step into the classroom, or before the teacher has even met them! Perhaps, for example, a student has a sibling who passed through the same classroom during a previous school year. Remembering a student who struggled academically or behaviorally in a previous year and placing similar expectations on his or her sibling is quite common. Teachers' lounge banter can influence perceptions as well, a factor to be cautious of.

Discussions between colleagues often center on difficulties faced in the classroom or difficult students in the classroom. In almost every school, there are "those students"—the ones all teachers know. Teachers recall all too well the hustle and bustle when they report for the new school year and hurry to gather performance, behavior, and attendance data and subgroup information (ethnicity, gender, free and reduced lunch, students with disabilities), as well as information from students' previous teachers. Although these labels are put in place to support students, they may have the unfortunate side effect of lowering a teacher's expectations.

There are other, even more controversial, reasons students face low expectations. Appearance and language use may be the first characteristics others use to set expectations. Finally, perhaps the most common factor in low expectations is socioeconomic status. While this information is certainly critical to establishing the starting point of students, the information should be used with a discerning eye, as bias can creep in without the teacher even realizing it.

Communicating high expectations for all students is an integral part of establishing conditions for rigor. If students don't feel they are expected to perform equally, the feeling will undoubtedly manifest in low self-esteem and lowered achievement. Unfortunately, it is not only others who set lower expectations for students of low socioeconomic status; research shows that these students themselves do not have high expectations for their own work (Odéen et al., 2013). These students may ultimately enter a state of learned helplessness. If students believe that they are likely to fail or underperform, they will likely not try at all. In other words, if they think they will not succeed, they will not put out the effort to do so (Jensen, 2009). Thus, it is crucial to set high expectations for all students and continuously communicate those expectations to them. It's a simple concept that can make all the difference in the world, especially for students who enter the classroom with low expectations for themselves.

Communicating high expectations for all students requires:

- A high degree of efficacy, a belief in one's ability to reach and teach any child

- A deep knowledge and love of content

- A toolkit of research-based content strategies

- A positive, supportive, and caring attitude toward students

Some foundational concepts to keep in mind:

- Convey respect and value to students.

- Deal with and respond to negative comments from one group of students to another.

- Provide additional opportunities to learn for low-expectancy students.

- Include all students in class discussions.

- Provide all students with opportunities to display achievement.

- Provide wait time for students who need additional time to process information.

- Hold all students responsible for answering difficult questions.

- Motivate and make personal connections with students.

- Involve students in personal goal setting.

Ways to Effectively Implement Communicating High Expectations for All Students

There are many ways to communicate high expectations for students. Your success in creating this condition for rigor begins with assessing your personal strengths and weaknesses as you explore the following recommendations from Marzano (2012).

Teacher Interactions with Students

- Verbal interaction: Use the following behaviors uniformly with all students to communicate your respect and to promote a positive classroom environment.

    - Using playful dialogue, taking care to avoid inappropriate humor or sarcasm

    - Addressing students in a manner *they* view as respectful

    - Acknowledging and expressing appreciation for students' involvement

    - Providing productive feedback that points out students' strengths and highlights any progress they have made

- Nonverbal interaction: In addition to verbal interaction, use the following nonverbal behaviors to communicate your respect for students.

    - Making eye contact in nonconfrontational ways

    - Smiling in a genuine way that shows you care

- Using discreet and appropriate proximity that doesn't invade a student's personal space but conveys a genuine interest in the student

- Making subtle gestures that are calming and do not overpower the student

- Ask cognitively complex questions that require students to make inferences, analyze information, evaluate conclusions, and utilize knowledge. All students should be asked these rigorous questions regardless of their background or achievement level. Expect all students to provide similar levels of evidence and support for answers. Each time a student makes a claim, require that grounds and backing be provided. If inferences are made to answer a question, require all students to explain their inferences.

- Provide support as needed to those students who may need help or encouragement to respond using the following techniques.

    - Question sequences: Memorize and rehearse the following protocol until you become skilled in employing it to probe incorrect answers (Marzano & Simms, 2014).

        1. When a student responds incorrectly, acknowledge the student's willingness and effort in responding.

        2. Next emphasize what was correct and what was incorrect in the student's response.

        3. If the answer was totally incorrect, identify the question that the incorrect response would have answered.

        4. Finally, provide support to help the student answer correctly, such as more time to think, hints and cues, a modified or restated original question, or asking a smaller part of the original question.

        5. At times, it may be appropriate to provide the correct answer and ask the student to elaborate on it, restate it in his or her own words, or provide an example (Marzano, 2012).

- Answer revision: This technique uses elaborative interrogation that encourages students to closely examine and think about their answers until they realize that their answer is not justifiable. Use questions like the following to encourage the student's thought process.

    1. How do you know that to be true?

    2. What evidence can you give to support your answer?

Common Mistakes to Avoid When Communicating High Expectations for All Students

Avoiding Students During Class Discussion

It may seem like you are protecting certain students by avoiding them during class discussions. Perhaps they do not often contribute correct answers and you do not want to embarrass them. However, the wrong answer is an opportunity to probe further and challenge students to meet the high expectations you have set for them. When students are routinely avoided in class discussions, they begin to believe that they are not held to the same expectations as others. As a result, they stop paying attention and often stop trying altogether. Conversely, if they expect to be called on and held to higher expectations, they are more likely to listen and be prepared to participate.

It may be necessary to spend some time tracking which students you call on or using a randomizing system to select students to answer questions. Often, avoiding students during class discussion is unintentional, and because of that, it is overlooked.

Not Providing All Students the Opportunity to Display Progress

Giving students opportunities to display progress reinforces confidence and spurs a desire to continue achieving. Aim to provide incremental opportunities for students to display achievement and opportunities to celebrate growth. For a template to use to track student growth, see figure 6.1.

Figure 6.1: Giving students opportunity to celebrate growth.

	Student Name					
Score						
4						
3						
2						
1						
0						
	Pretest	Formative Assessment #1	Formative Assessment #2	Formative Assessment #3	Formative Assessment #4	Post Test

More Ways to Hold High Expectations for Students as Shared by Experienced Educators

Dream Boards

When students don't come from families with big dreams about where their children are going to attend college, they need permission to dream big and encouragement from their teachers. Dream boards are twelve-by-eighteen-inch pieces of construction paper on which students create a visual of their dreams and hopes—what they want to be when they grow up, where they want to go to college, what kind of house they want to live in, and where they want to travel. All of the dream boards are posted in the hallways of a school during the year and become a key part of motivating everyone (McEwan, 2002). For a sample dream board, see figure 6.2 (page 106).

Figure 6.2: Sample dream board.

Source: McEwan, 2002.

Personal Achievement Goals

Once students have dreamed big dreams, expect them to set individual academic goals based on standards. Figure 6.3 displays a sample student goal-setting form.

Here's some advice from award-winning principal Lillie Jesse (reprinted by permission).

Many students in low-income areas come from homes like mine as a child, where no family member has ever attended college. One of my critical goals as an instructional leader was to plant the idea of attending college or achieving a high-paying career in the minds of students early on. Our primary grade initiative took place in kindergarten. The week-long event was called Kindergarten to College. Every faculty member wore a

Figure 6.3: Sample student goal-setting form.

Directions: Think of the school-related goal you would like to achieve during the upcoming school year. Write down the actions you will take during the year to achieve this goal.

My Goal:

To score proficient or higher on the California Standards English Language Arts Test Grade 4

What I Will Do to Reach My Goal:

I will pay attention to my teacher during instruction.

I will help my classmates learn by working together with them in cooperative groups.

I will do my homework every day.

I will go to tutoring every day.

I will read a book of my own choosing every week and aim to read one-half million words during the school year.

I will look for the main events of the plot and their causes. I will study the characters' personalities and try to figure out why they do the things they do.

I will try to figure out what the author's specific purpose is in writing a story or article.

I will try to figure out who the speaker is or who the narrator is in everything I read.

---

sweatshirt from their college and talked with students about that college and why they attended it. Parents were encouraged to take college field trips with their children.

In another initiative, we took all of the fifth graders to the Virginia Tech campus and continued to nurture the idea that college was attainable if students studied and did their best. The buses left the parking lot at 4 a.m., but every student was there on time. This is how to foster collective efficacy among teachers, students, and parents. You will have your own ideas, but the goal is to plant the seeds of academic achievement early and tend to them often.

Opportunities to Teach and Reinforce Conative Skills

As you recall, conative skills enable students to make proper real-world decisions. Conative skills combine how a student feels (emotion) and what a student knows (intelligence) in order to come to a conclusion or resolution. The development of conative skills aids the creation of rigorous learning environments.

Cultivating a Growth Mindset

This strategy makes way for great opportunities to cultivate a growth mindset. When teachers or students believe that ability is fixed and cannot increase, it influences engagement and learning (Dweck, 2000). The simple belief that hard work and effort can grow ability has the potential to change the path of a struggling student. A simple adjustment in the language you use may be all it takes.

Try to avoid comforting language that may imply the student is not good at a task or area of study or that his or her other strengths somehow make up for a shortcoming (e.g., "Not all of us are good at math, but you are such a talented artist!"). Instead, provide reinforcement that supports the effort and guides students to choose appropriate strategies and grow their positive attitudes. Providing prompt, actionable, and task-specific feedback helps students believe in their own growth (Jensen, 2009).

> "Mary, I know that this math concept seems really hard right now. I hope you see the improvement that I see. This was a new topic, something that no one was introduced to before this year. You have been able to quickly learn and apply the process for calculation. The next area we need to focus on is applying the process to real-world problems. Pay close attention to what the problem is asking. You got this far by not giving up. If you keep pushing yourself and asking for help when you need it, you will get there!"

Such feedback helps students determine when they need to take action, what they need to do, and how to make improvements.

Cultivating Resiliency

The conative skill of resiliency pairs nicely with cultivating a growth mindset. Students who lack belief in their ability to grow or achieve often give up when a task becomes too difficult. Some classroom behaviors may even support this by lightening the load for certain students, such as challenging only a small portion of students with more complex content. Such load adjustments are likely unnecessary unless they have been recommended in a 504 plan, Individual Education Plan (IEP), or other similar legal document. Instead of telling a student he or she has worked hard enough and should not feel bad for not accomplishing a task, encourage persistence. Provide words of encouragement to work through the struggle. If students are struggling to complete a task, we need to figure out where they hit the wall and then support them to be able to complete it. Supporting and encouraging resiliency teaches students to problem solve and work through a task without giving up, an important classroom skill and an even more important life skill.

Examples and Nonexamples of Communicating High Expectations for All Students

Elementary Example

In this example, when students are not in group discussion, a fourth-grade teacher uses name cards to select students to answer questions. Name cards allow her to randomly select students and avoid only choosing students that she believes will have the right answer. In addition, she places checkmarks on an erasable seating chart (figures 6.4 and 6.5, pages 110 and 111) to indicate how often students responded to questions.

Figure 6.4: Erasable seating chart.

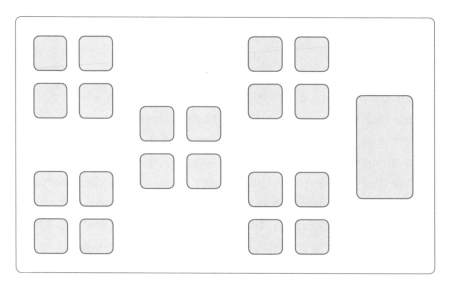

While engaging the whole group in a discussion about the story they are reading, she asks students to think about the sequence of events.

"Class, I want you to think about the story we have been reading. Today, we will be focusing on sequencing. Each of you should be able to identify the order in which key events occurred in the text. I will call on one of you randomly to tell me the order the events occurred."

When she selects a student from the cards to share the sequence of events, the student struggles to respond. Instead of moving on, she asks the student to review what happened first. The student is able to share that detail. She then asks the student what came next and directs her back to the text to find the answer.

"Aaliyah, I see that you are having a little trouble remembering the sequence of events from the text. Let's try this a different way. Can you tell me the very first thing that happened in the text? How about what happened next? If you need to, you can refer back to the text to help you out."

The student is able to share that detail. She then asks the student what came next and directs her back to the text to find the answer. When the student looks back at the story, she is able to recall the sequence of events and correctly answer the rest of the question.

The result is that all students expect to be called on and know that they are all held to the same high expectations.

Figure 6.5: Tracking student participation with erasable seating chart.

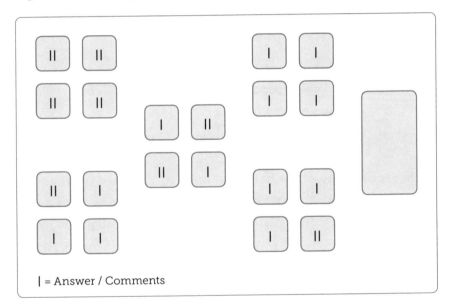

| = Answer / Comments

Elementary Nonexample

In a fourth-grade classroom similar to the previous example, the teacher spends a lot of time planning out her questions. They increase in complexity throughout the lesson. As they get more complex, she notices that fewer students volunteer to answer.

"Class, think about the text that we are currently reading. Listen carefully to my questions and raise your hand if you have an answer."

Beyond that, she notices that on first try, some students are unable to answer correctly. She seldom calls on students who do not raise their hands, especially students she has put on the spot in the past who have been unable to answer the question.

In this case, she has called on the student from the previous example. When the student struggles, she asks if anyone would like to help her. She gives the student an opportunity to call on another student from the class. She is directed to only call on a student who is raising his or her hand.

"Aaliyah, I see that you are having trouble answering the question. It's OK. Look around the room and select someone who's hand is up to help you out."

The teacher is unaware of her behavior, but it has resulted in a handful of students who know that they do not need to participate beyond a certain point. It has also resulted in frustration from students who would like to attempt an answer but are regularly overlooked.

Secondary Example

In a tenth-grade literature class, students often participate in colorful discussion about the text. In this example, the class is discussing the book *Flowers for Algernon*. They have been asked if the experiment conducted on Charlie Gordon was ethical. They have shared opinions in class discussion but are all responsible for producing their own arguments.

"OK, class, we have been discussing the book *Flowers for Algernon*. You have all been able to discuss as a group if the experiment conducted on Charlie was ethical. Now, I want to hear your personal thoughts and what textual evidence you used to come to that conclusion.

"Anthony, you claim that the experiment was ethical, but I need more. What evidence from the story shows that it helped people?"

When one student states that the experiment was ethical because it helped other people, the teacher asks him to elaborate.

"What evidence from the story shows that it helped people?" After examining his reasoning, the student shares that he still believes that the experiment was ethical. "It may not have helped anyone in the long run, but Charlie enjoyed being smart. And, he agreed to the experiment in the first place."

By asking the student to return to the text and produce a claim, the teacher communicated that he was being held to the same high expectations as the rest of the class.

Secondary Nonexample

In a classroom like the one above, students are given the same task. In this case, the student's answer about the ethics of the experiment is accepted.

> "Class, we have been reading *Flowers for Algernon*. Now that you have had a moment to speak with others, I'd like to hear from individuals. Anthony, let's start with you. Tell us your claim and the textual evidence that supports it."
>
> "I think that the experiment was ethical because it helped people."
>
> Anthony's answer is accepted by the teacher, and she moves on. "Terrific job, Anthony. Would anyone else like to share their opinion?"

In accepting Anthony's answer so readily, this teacher indirectly sends the message that thoughts will not be challenged and that not all students will be required to substantiate their claims with evidence from the text. She has missed an opportunity to create a culture in which all students understand that their answers will be challenged and that they can't expect other students to fill in the gaps in their answers.

A Middle School Math and Science Teacher Shares How a "Lost Cause" Becomes a Respected Member of the School Community

Previous teachers had labeled Sam a lost cause, and his classmates followed the teachers' lead. Consequently, Sam spent a good share of the year in the office for behavioral problems. Here's how the math and science teacher describes Sam, before and after high expectations (adapted with permission from McEwan, 2009):

> Sam was a learning support student who was very bright, a bit quirky, and the most disorganized student I had ever met. But his learning support teacher, my partner who teaches language arts and social studies, and I made Sam our personal project for the year. We would not give up on that kid. Everybody stayed on him, but in a very positive and caring way. We locked arms and would not let him get through our blockade of care, support, and instruction. When one of us got frustrated, one of the

others would read a poem aloud that Sam had written on the back of a math assignment he didn't turn in. When somebody else got discouraged, I would tell them something amazing that Sam had just done. By the end of the year we all loved that kid. The world has to have people who think outside the box. Sam lived outside the box. But he was always interesting and thought provoking. Both my partner and I appreciated his intelligence and gave him a forum where he could speak out in class. Interestingly enough, by the end of the year, not only was he getting all of his homework and assignments turned in, the kids in the class respected him.

Monitoring for the Desired Result of Communicating High Expectations for All Students

Monitoring for this strategy requires you to determine whether students feel you have high expectations for them. When you have communicated high expectations for all students effectively, your treatment of students, regardless of background or achievement level, will remain consistent and unbiased.

- Listen as students respond to verbal interactions to ensure that such interactions help students feel valued and increase personal expectations.

- Observe students during nonverbal interactions to verify that they feel equally valued and are participating in the lesson.

- Listen as students respond to questions to ensure they are participating and attempting to answer cognitively complex questions.

- Observe students after asking questions to monitor if they are attempting to work with the content and if they expect to share their reasoning and support for their claims.

- Create or use a tool to track response rates to ensure all students ask and answer questions with the same frequency and depth.

- Watch students to see if they all anticipate the same consistent questioning and probing of incorrect answers and appear comfortable revising their thinking without fear of negative feedback.

Please see the proficiency scale in figure 6.6 to determine your level of proficiency within this strategy.

Figure 6.6: Student proficiency scale for maintaining high expectations. The proficiency scale identifies phases of implementation regarding the strategy. The "Desired Result" articulates the desired outcome of using the strategy, while "Emerging" and "Fundamental" represent a developmental progression in its use.

Condition	Emerging	Fundamental	Desired Result
Communicating high expectations for all students	Students listen to the perspective of their classmates. Students participate in class. Students respond to feedback to reframe their negative speak. Student artifacts show the same expectancy levels.	Students treat each other with respect. Students are willing to attempt challenging tasks. Students avoid negative speak about themselves. Students articulate their hopes and goals to the teacher and to other students.	Students do not tolerate disrespectful behavior from one another. Students are willing to take risks in front of the teacher and their classmates. Students identify and give feedback when others speak negatively about themselves. Students actively work toward their goals and seek guidance and help from their teacher and other students.

Scaffold and Extend to Meet Student Needs

You may need to make adjustments to reach the desired result with each student. Your adaptations will depend on the technique you are implementing and should provide extra support, scaffolding, or extension that students may need in order to reach the desired result.

Scaffolding

- For students who may not benefit from, or who may misinterpret, verbal interactions, use nonverbal interactions to communicate value and respect.

- Conference with students to clear any misconceptions or miscommunication of nonverbal behavior and mutually determine a way to communicate value and respect.

- Post questions to a class website or otherwise provide questions prior to asking them in class so that all students may be prepared during the activity.

- Provide a "think sheet," which provides guiding questions for students to refer to while making inferences and claims.

- Privately inform students who do not volunteer that you want them to answer more questions and that you are planning to begin calling on them more.

- Ask students to revise specific parts of their response instead of the whole response to questions.

Extending

- Ask students to develop phrases that express appreciation, value, and respect that could be used in class.

- Ask students to develop nonverbal gestures that express appreciation, value, and respect that could be used by all.

- Ask students to explain how their thinking changed once they were asked to provide evidence and support for their answer.

- Check in with students to see how they feel about being called on to answer questions more often.

- Ask students to identify similarities and differences between their answers and their partner's answers.

Conclusion

The goal of this guide is to enable teachers to become more effective in establishing the conditions for rigor in their classrooms. To determine if you have indeed become more effective in practicing these strategies, you will need to gather information from your students as well as solicit feedback from your peers, coaches, or supervisor to find someone willing to embark on this learning journey with you. Make it your goal to consistently engage in meaningful self-reflection on your use of the five strategies described in the guide.

If you acquire nothing else from this guide, let it be the importance of *monitoring*. Implementing these strategies well is not enough. The tipping point in your level of expertise and your students' achievement is monitoring for the desired effect of each strategy and adapting your process to ensure that you are consistently reaching the desired result. Your goal is the desired result: evidence that your students are moving in the direction of more cognitively complex content while at the same time becoming more autonomous and self-managed in their learning.

To be more effective, think about implementation as a three-step process:

1. Implement the strategies using your energy and creativity to adapt the various techniques and approaches in this guide.

2. Monitor for the desired result while you are implementing the strategies to determine whether the strategy is effective with students. Check to see if your students are moving to higher levels of thinking while at the same time becoming more independent learners.

3. If, as a result of your monitoring, you realize that your efforts are not proving adequate to achieve your goal, seek out ways to change or adapt your approach by either scaffolding or extending so that all students are making progress.

Although you can certainly read this guide and gain expertise independently, the process will be more beneficial if you read and work through its contents with colleagues.

Reflection and Discussion Questions

Use the following reflection and discussion questions during a team meeting or even as food for thought prior to a meeting with your coach, mentor, or supervisor:

1. How have the conditions for rigor in your classroom changed as a result of reading and implementing the strategies in this book?

2. What ways have you found to modify and enhance the strategies to scaffold and extend your approaches to establishing the conditions for rigor?

3. What was your biggest challenge in terms of implementing the strategies?

4. How would you describe the changes in your students' motivation and engagement, particularly low-engagement students?

5. What will you do to share what you have learned with colleagues at your grade level or in your department?

The best way to increase your instructional expertise is to implement, monitor, and analyze your students' learning growth. Years of research science have shown that when the five strategies in this guide are effectively implemented, student achievement and learning will increase, but only when the strategies are implemented with the artful teaching judgment and experience displayed by effective teachers. It is this masterful combination of the art and science of teaching that creates the most rigorous learning environments, the most satisfaction for teachers, and the best results for students.

Appendix A

TEMPLATES

Chapter 2: Template for Determining Necessity for Rules and Procedures

Rules and procedures are necessary throughout the day. In chapter 2, several instances were listed, many of which are often overlooked. Use the space provided to determine times throughout the school day that will require specific rules or procedures. It may be helpful to return to this document after the first weeks of school to revise it based on observations you have made. Use the document titled "Planning the Steps to Teach Rules and Procedures" to document how you will teach each rule or procedure you deem necessary.

Time of Day or Activity that Necessitates Rules or Procedures	List the Rule or Procedure Necessary

Visit www.LearningSciences.com to download this reproducible.

Chapter 2: Template for Planning the Steps to Teach Rules and Procedures

List the rule or procedure for which you are planning:

_____

Record your plans for using the steps of teaching rules and procedures in the space provided below.

Explain the rule or procedure: How will you define and describe the rule/procedure? What rationale will you share with students?
Rehearse the rule or procedure: In what activity will your students participate in order to practice the rule or procedure?
Reinforce the rule or procedure: What specific activities will students use to turn new rules and procedures into habits?

Visit www.LearningSciences.com to download this reproducible.

Chapter 2: Template for Organizing Physical Space

Sketch the dimensions of your classroom. Remember to include spaces for doorways and restrooms. Use the grid to organize your physical space. Below are some examples of scenarios to consider.

Traffic: Are doorways and restrooms easily accessible? Where will materials be kept so that they can be accessed with minimal effort? Are students able to easily line up?

Reaching all students: Is the furniture arranged in such a way that you can reach close proximity of each student in a timely manner? Considering each activity that will take place, are all students visible to you at all times? In turn, are you visible to them?

Potential distractions: Are any students at risk of facing high-traffic areas (such as windows facing a busy hallway)? Which direction are classroom computers facing, and do they pose a risk of disruption?

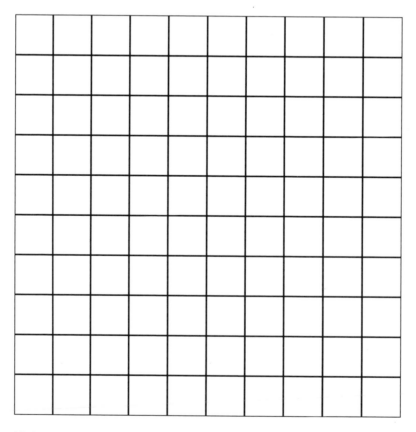

Visit www.LearningSciences.com to download this reproducible.

Chapter 3: Template for Graduated Actions

Use this document as an example or template for posting graduated actions. It is helpful for students to know and recognize when these actions are being implemented in order for them to be able to adjust their behavior.

Elementary Example

	If I look you in the eye for more than five seconds, consider adjusting your behavior.
	If you continue to not follow a rule or procedure, I will move closer to you. When this happens, it is VERY important that you fix your behavior immediately, so that there are no further consequences.
	If you and I need to have a private conversation, it means that you have disrupted the lesson. When we speak, be prepared for further consequences.
	I hope that the behavior will not continue, but if it does, I will speak to you in front of your peers and share further consequences such as removal from your group, phone call home, or a visit to the principal.

Elementary Example

	Visual Warning: Eye contact is a silent message sent to inform you that your behavior is not acceptable and must be corrected.
	Proximity: If your behavior continues to be unacceptable, expect that I will move closer to you. This is another silent message, and I expect immediate correction of behavior.
	Private Conversation: If unacceptable behavior continues, expect a private conversation, which will result in appropriate consequences.
	Public Conversation: If behavior escalates to the need for public conversation, it will result in more severe consequences, including but not limited to moving your seat, behavior referral, or required phone call home.

Visit www.LearningSciences.com to download this reproducible.

Chapter 4: Template for Making Connections

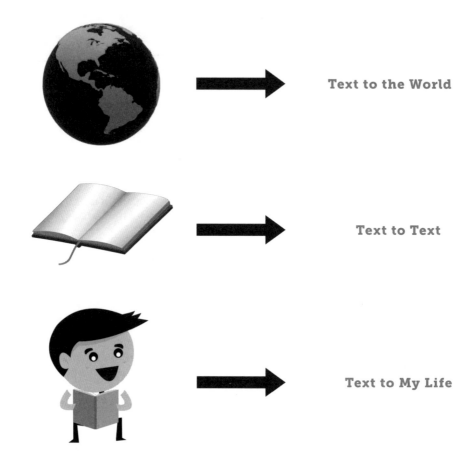

Visit www.LearningSciences.com to download this reproducible.

Ways to Respectfully Disagree

I see it differently because _____.

Is your position that _____?

I understand what you are saying. Could I just add to that a little bit?

You make a good point, but _____.

Can you explain that a little more? I would like to better understand why you feel that way.

I appreciate your opinion, but I respectfully disagree because

_____.

Visit www.LearningSciences.com to download this reproducible.

Chapter 5: Template for Weekly Student Interaction Schedule

Class:

Period:

Student Name	Planned Interaction	Monday	Tuesday	Wednesday	Thursday	Friday

Visit www.LearningSciences.com to download this reproducible.

Chapter 5: Template for Daily Self-Reflection

What opportunities did I have to enforce positive and negative consequences?

Which of my actions reflected positive reinforcements (list or tally)?	Which of my actions reflected negative reinforcements (list or tally)?

How might I further plan to balance my interactions in the future?

Visit www.LearningSciences.com to download this reproducible.

Chapter 5: Template for Six-Word Autobiography

Use the following reproducible document with your students. Cut along the dotted lines to distribute template to students.

Write your autobiography in six words:

_____   _____   _____

_____   _____   _____.

Write your autobiography in six words:

_____   _____   _____

_____   _____   _____.

Write your autobiography in six words:

_____   _____   _____

_____   _____   _____.

Write your autobiography in six words:

_____   _____   _____

_____   _____   _____.

Visit www.LearningSciences.com to download this reproducible.

Chapter 6: Template for Communicating High Expectations for All Students

Fill out the T-chart. Think about the students in your class. Who are the students that you anticipate will do well this year? Who are the students you anticipate will struggle?

This allows you to plan for adaptations needed to help all students. Low-expectancy students are determined by our perceptions. It is important to identify these students due to the fact that our perceptions often dictate our actions.

Students who I believe will do well	Students who I believe will not do well

Action Step

What will you do to ensure high expectations for all students?

Visit www.LearningSciences.com to download this reproducible.

RESOURCES FOR THE ESSENTIALS FOR ACHIEVING RIGOR MODEL

Full resources for the Essentials for Achieving Rigor model may be retrieved from www.learningsciences.com/Essentials.

The Essentials for Achieving Rigor Book Series

Cowritten by Robert J. Marzano and Learning Sciences International consultants, each book in the Essentials series provides practical classroom strategies that teachers can put to immediate use to move students toward the higher-order thinking skills required by rigorous new standards. The authors provide techniques for implementing and monitoring critical instructional strategies, recommendations for adapting lessons to ensure that all students understand the content, day-to-day examples, and lists of common mistakes to avoid.

The series includes *Examining Similarities & Differences; Identifying Critical Content; Examining Reasoning; Recording & Representing Knowledge; Revising Knowledge; Processing New Information; Engaging in Cognitively Complex Tasks; Practicing Skills, Strategies, & Processes; Creating & Using Learning Targets & Performance Scales; Organizing for Learning;* and *Monitoring the Learning Environment.*

Other Resources

White Paper
Marzano, R. J., & Toth, M. D. (2014). *Teaching for rigor: A call for a critical instructional shift.* Retrieved from www.marzanocenter.com/files /Teaching-for-Rigor-20140318.pdf

Demonstration Schools for Rigor Resources

Visit www.learningsciences.com/services/demonstration-schools-for
-rigor for information about Demonstration Schools for Rigor.

Case Studies

- Princeton School District, Minnesota

- Acreage Pines Elementary, Florida

- Calusa Elementary, Florida

- Glades Area 3 Schools, Florida

Tools and Technology

The LSI Growth Tracker

The LSI Growth Tracker is an easy-to-use online tool for teachers' professional growth and collaboration around instructional strategies. In addition
to supporting instructional coaching and peer coaching, the tracker makes
professional learning visible while helping teachers grow (and helping each
other grow) in a safe, evaluation-free zone. Visit www.learningsciences.com
/lsitracker/growth-tracker for more information.

LSI Standards Tracker

Equipped with the standards from all fifty states for K–12 ELA and math,
the LSI Standards Tracker deconstructs the standards into learning targets
with student success criteria, which allows K–12 teachers to easily collect student evidence of learning during instruction. This robust web-based platform
then enables teachers to share data with other educators, promoting a unique
blend of calibration and professional growth. Visit www.learningsciences
.com/lsitracker/standards-tracker for more information.

RigorWalk

RigorWalk™ helps school leadership teams gain powerful insight into
instruction and leadership. During a RigorWalk, Learning Sciences consultants facilitate interviews with the school leadership team, walk the school,
and conduct an on-site analysis to collect information about the pillars of rigor.
Visit www.learningsciences.com/solutions/rigorwalk for more information.

Quick Reference Guides

- Rigor/Standards-Based Teaching Map Quick Reference Guide

- Taxonomy Crosswalk Quick Reference Guide

- Standards-Based Learning Targets and Performance Scales Quick Reference Guide[6]

---

6 Available in 2017.

References

Bandura, A. (1991). Self-efficacy mechanism in physiological activation of health-promoting behavior. In J. Madden IV (Ed.), *Neurobiology of learning, emotion and affect* (pp. 229–270). New York: Raven.

Bradley, R. H., & Corwyn, R. F. (2002). Socioeconomic status and child development. *Annual Review of Psychology, 53*, 371–399.

Council of State Governments Justice Center & Public Policy Research Institute. (2011). *Breaking schools' rules: A statewide study of how school discipline relates to students' success and juvenile justice involvement.* Retrieved from https://csgjusticecenter.org/wp-content/uploads/2012/08/Breaking_Schools_Rules _Report_Final.pdf

Dweck, C. S. (2000). *Self-theories: Their roles in motivation, personality, and development.* New York: Psychology Press.

Elias, M. (2015). *Using humor in the classroom.* Retrieved from www.edutopia.org /blog/using-humor-in-the-classroom-maurice-elias

Fabelo, T., Thompson, M., Plotkin, M., Carmichael, D., Marchbanks III, M., & Booth, E. (2017). Breaking school rules: A statewide study of how school discipline relates to students' success and juvenile justice involvement. Retrieved from https://csgjusticecenter.org/wp-content/uploads/2012/08/Breaking School Rules Report Final.pdf

Fredericks, J. A., Blumenfeld, P. C., & Paris, A. H. (2004). School engagement: Potential of the concept, state of the evidence. *Review of Educational Research, 74*(1), 49–109.

Good, T. L., & Brophy, J. E. (2003). *Looking in classrooms* (9th ed.). Boston: Allyn & Bacon.

Gottlieb, D. J., Beiser, A. S., & O'Connor, G. T. (1995). Poverty, race, and medication use are correlates of asthma hospitalization rates: A small area analysis in Boston. *Chest, 108*(1), 28–35.

Hiroto, D. S., & Seligman, M. E. (1975). Generality of learned helplessness in man. *Journal of Personality and Social Psychology, 31*(2), 311–327.

Indiana State University. (2007). *National high school student engagement survey by IU reveals unengaged students* [Press release]. Bloomington Indiana State

University. Retrieved from www.indiana.edu/~soenews/news/news1172622996
.html

Jensen, E. (2009). *Teaching with poverty in mind: What being poor does to kids'
brains and what schools can do about it.* Alexandria, VA: ASCD.

Jensen, E. (2013). How poverty affects classroom engagement. *Educational
Leadership, 70*(8), 24–30.

Kounin, J. S. (1970). *Discipline and group management in classrooms.* Indiana
University: Holt, Rinehart, and Winston of Canada, Ltd.

Marzano, R. J. (2003). *Classroom management that works: Research-based strategies
for every teacher.* Alexandria, VA: ASCD.

Marzano, R. J. (2007). *The art and science of teaching: A comprehensive framework
for effective instruction.* Alexandria, VA: ASCD.

Marzano, R. J. (2012). *Becoming a reflective teacher.* Bloomington, IN: Marzano
Research Laboratory.

Marzano, R. J., Carbaugh, B., Rutherford, A., & Toth, M. D. (2014). *Marzano Center
teacher observation protocol for the 2014 Marzano teacher evaluation model.*
West Palm Beach, FL: Learning Sciences International.

Marzano, R. J., Gaddy, B. B., Foseid, M. C., Foseid, M. P., & Marzano, J. S. (2005). *A
handbook for classroom management that works.* Alexandria, VA: ASCD.

Marzano, R. J., & Marzano, J. S. (2003). The key to classroom management.
Educational Leadership, 61(1), 6–13. Retrieved from http://www.ascd.org
/publications/educational-leadership/sept03/vol61/num01/The-Key-to
-Classroom-Management.aspx

Marzano, R. J., & Marzano, J. S. (2015). *Managing the inner world of teaching:
Emotions, interpretations, and actions.* Bloomington, IN: Marzano Research
Laboratory.

Marzano, R. J., Marzano, J. S., & Pickering, D. J. (2003). *Classroom management that
works: Research-based strategies for every teacher.* Alexandria, VA: Association
for Supervision and Curriculum Development.

Marzano, R. J., Pickering, D. J., & Heflebower, T. (2011). *The highly engaged
classroom.* Bloomington, IN: Marzano Research Laboratory.

Marzano, R. J., & Toth, M. D. (2013). *Teacher evaluation that makes a difference: A new
model for teacher growth and student achievement.* Alexandria, VA: ASCD.

Marzano, R. J., & Simms, J. A. (2014). *Questioning sequences in the classroom*. Bloomington, IN: Marzano Research Laboratory.

Marzano, R. J., Yanoski, D. C., Hoegh, J. K., Simms, J. A., Heflebower, T., & Warrick, P. B. (2013). *Using Common Core standards to enhance classroom instruction & assessment*. Bloomington, IN: Marzano Research Laboratory.

McEwan, E. K. (2002). *The ten traits of highly effective teachers*. Thousand Oaks, CA: Corwin.

McEwan-Adkins, E. K. (2012). *Collaborative teacher literacy teams, K–6: Connecting professional growth to student achievement*. Bloomington, IN: Solution Tree Press.

Menyuk, P. (1980). Effect of persistent otitis media on language development. *Annals of otology, rhinology & laryngology supplement, 89*(3), 257–263.

Moore, C., Garst., L. H., Marzano, R. J., Kennedy, E., & Senn, D. (2015). *Creating and using learning targets & performance scales: How teachers make better instructional decisions*. West Palm Beach, FL: Learning Sciences International.

Mouton, S. G., Hawkins, J., McPherson, R. H., & Copley, J. (1996). School attachment: Perspectives of low-attached high school students. *Educational Psychology, 16*(3), 297–305.

Noguera, P. (2012). The achievement gap and the schools we need: Creating the conditions where race and class no longer predict student achievement. *In Motion Magazine*. Retrieved from http://www.inmotionmagazine.com/er12/pn_achvgap.html

Odéen, M., Westerlund, H., Theorell, T., Leineweber, C., Eriksen, H. R., & Ursin, H. (2013). Expectations, socioeconomic status, and self-rated health: Use of the simplified TOMCATS questionnaire. *International Journal of Behavioral Medicine, 20*(2), 242–251.

Reeve, J. (2006). Extrinsic rewards and inner motivation. In C. Evertson, C. M. Weinstein & C. S. Weinstein (Eds.), *Handbook of classroom management: Research, practice, and contemporary issues* (pp. 645–664). Mahwah, NJ: Erlbaum.

Saphier, J., & Gower, R. (1997). *The skillful teacher: Building your teaching skills*. Carlisle, MA: Research for Better Teaching.

Sargent, J. D., Brown, M. J., Freeman, J. L., Bailey, A., Goodman, D., & Freeman Jr., D. H. (1995). Childhood lead poisoning in Massachusetts communities: Its association with sociodemographic and housing characteristics. *American Journal of Public Health, 85*(4), 528–534.

Sousa, D. A. (2011). *How the brain learns* (4th ed.). Thousand Oaks, CA: Corwin Press.

Sprick, R., & Baldwin, K. (2009). *CHAMPS: A proactive & positive approach to classroom management.* Eugene, OR: Pacific Northwest Publishing.

Wanzer, M. (2002). Use of humor in the classroom: The good, the bad, and the not-so-funny things that teachers say and do. In J. L. Chesebro & J. C. McCroskey (Eds.), *Communication for Teachers* (pp. 116–126). Boston, MA: Allyn and Bacon. Retrieved from https://www.uab.edu/Communicationstudies/richmond_files/Richmond%20Humor%20in%20Classroom.pdf

Wong, H. K., & Wong, R. T. (2001). *The first days of school: How to be an effective teacher.* Mountain View, CA: Harry K. Wong Publications, Inc.

Wubbels, T., Brekelmans, M., van Tartwijk, J., & Admiral, W. (1999). Interpersonal relationships between teachers and students in the classroom. In H. C. Waxman & H. J. Walberg (Eds.), *New directions for teaching practice and research* (pp. 151–170). Berkeley, CA: McCutchan Publishing Corp.

Wubbels, T., & Levy, J. (1993). *Do you know what you look like? Interpersonal relationships in education.* London: Falmer Press.

Index

Information found in figures and tables is indicated by (f) and (t), respectively, following the page number.

Notes

Notes